ANXIETY IN THE DIGITAL AGE

NAVIGATING MODERN STRESSORS

this book. Neither directly nor indirectly.

INTRODUCTION TO THE DIGITAL AGE

You are living in an extraordinary time. The digital age is when technology is integrated into practically every aspect of your existence. This book takes you on a trip to discover how this new world affects something very intimate and frequently hidden - your mental health.

Consider this. How recently did you check your phone? Have you gone through social media? Have you sent an email? These seemingly insignificant and ordinary behaviors are like threads in the great tapestry of the digital world. And although they provide indisputable benefits, they also introduce complications.

You've probably felt the subtle, occasionally overpowering worry that may accompany continual connectivity. It's like a buzz in your mind, a constant hum of notifications, updates, likes, and shares. But how does your continual digital presence impact your mental health?

This book will go over exactly that. You are not alone in experiencing the gentle uneasiness of an endless flood of information and the more profound effects of digital overload. The digital age is a shared experience, and its impacts on mental health are becoming increasingly apparent.

The goal of this book is not just to study these effects but also to provide you with a map to help you navigate this digital terrain. You'll learn about real-life experiences, scientific findings, and practical solutions for understanding and managing the anxiety of living in a digital environment.

Consider this your guide, a source of empathy and understanding in a world where your digital life and mental health are intricately interwoven. You are not a passive observer of the digital age; you are an active participant in molding your mental health inside it.

CHAPTER 1: UNDERSTANDING ANXIETY IN THE DIGITAL WORLD

Defining Anxiety

Consider yourself standing on the edge of a precipice, your heart racing, your palms sweating, and your breath rapid and shallow. This is your body's natural reaction to a perceived threat - a primordial impulse designed to keep you safe. Imagine feeling this way in the middle of a normal day, not on the edge of a precipice. This is called anxiousness.

Anxiety is more than a single emotion or a brief period of nervousness. It's far more complicated than that. Consider it a multidimensional tapestry of emotions, finely woven and consistently present, frequently arising even when there is no evident or immediate danger. It's similar to an extremely sensitive alarm system within you, one that emits warnings and alarms, instilling panic and terror even when the harm isn't genuine or immediate. This alert can be set off by the tiniest of cues, leaving you perplexed as to why your body and mind are reacting so strongly.

Anxiety is, at its foundation, your body's natural, programmed response to stress. It's a primal sense, deeply ingrained in our psyche, a dread of what's to come. Consider yourself on the verge of a new experience, such as the first day of a new job, preparing to speak at a public event, or meeting someone for the first time. While these events appear harmless, they might send off internal alarm bells, causing a rush of worry. It's a natural human reaction to the unknown or the difficult things of life. Anxiety serves as a signal in these situations, a form of mental and physiological preparedness for prospective obstacles.

However, worry's true intricacy comes in its propensity to transition from a normal, adaptive response to something more consuming and permanent. Fear and apprehension don't leave some people easily; they remain and intensify, becoming a persistent, overwhelming presence. When anxiety reaches this level, it begins to interfere with daily living, making even simple, ordinary chores appear intimidating and overwhelming. This is the point at which it becomes an anxiety disorder.

Anxiety disorders are distinguished not only by the intensity of these symptoms but also by their persistence and ability to exert control over one's life. It's as if the internal alarm system is constantly functioning, creating an almost constant sense of heightened alertness and dread rather than only responding to certain stressors or threats. This can cause various physical and mental symptoms, ranging from sleep difficulties and difficulty concentrating to emotions of restlessness and dread.

Anxiety can manifest itself in a variety of physical and emotional manifestations, each as unique as your life experiences. For some, it seems like a churning sensation in the stomach, a kind of disquiet that twists and turns within, upsetting your thoughts and your physical well-being. Others experience anxiety as a racing heart, a constant hammering that feels like it's trying to break free from their chest. It's more than a symbolic 'heart skipping a beat' in a panic attack; it's a continual, physical rapidity in your heartbeat, sometimes accompanied by shortness of breath, making calm seem like a distant dream.

Then, there's the mental side of worry, characterized by a flurry of thoughts that refuse to settle. It's like an inside hurricane, with ideas swirling about in a chaotic circle, each triggering the next, never allowing you to relax or find a quiet moment. Worries about the future, repeating previous mistakes, or a barrage of what-ifs and worst-case scenarios are all examples of these thoughts. This constant brain chatter can be tiring, leaving you exhausted and unable to concentrate on the task.

Anxiety is profoundly personal, and its appearance varies greatly from person to person. A simple ripple in one person's life may become a tidal wave in another's. Despite these distinctions, one thing that all people who suffer from anxiety have in common is that it has a significant influence on their daily lives. Anxiety may elevate mundane chores to Herculean proportions. Simple decisions become complicated and laden with uncertainty. Activities that should be enjoyable or relaxing may instead be tainted with a sense of discomfort or worry.

This affects moments that should be filled with peace or joy. Imagine looking forward to a social occasion, only to be bombarded by nervous thoughts as the event approaches, draining the excitement and joy from the encounter. Consider the simple act of going to bed, which becomes a nightly battle for many people as worry turns the darkness into a microphone for anxieties and fears.

Anxiety's insidious nature implies that it affects more than simply life's big moments or visible obstacles. It penetrates into minor, daily moments, tinting them with worry and unease. The world can seem more intimidating, and you may find yourself holding back, avoiding experiences, and narrowing your environment in an attempt to calm your anxiety.

THE DIGITAL CONNECTION

Consider this scenario: you pick up your phone for a short check, and before you realize it, hours have passed. Your connection to the world is constant and unforgiving in the digital age. While technology and social media are amazing at connecting us, they have fundamentally changed the way you experience and perceive worry.

Always on
Consider how frequently your phone vibrates with notifications, each functioning as a little hook that slowly pulls you back into the digital sphere. This constant flood of signals, from social media updates to business emails, creates an infinite loop in which each buzz and beep competes for your attention. It's as if these digital nudges have established their own rhythm in your life, which isn't easy to break, leaving you feeling linked to an intangible yet pervasive digital world.

This never-ending loop of connectivity can be exhausting. It's not simply the number of these interruptions but their variety and perceived importance. A message from a friend, a family member's update, a work-related email, or even a notification about an upcoming sale merges into a torrent of digital noise that can be difficult to filter. As a result, there is a constant sense of being 'on,' of being ready to respond, react, or participate at a moment's notice.

In this stage, the lines that have historically divided different aspects of your life begin to blur. Work does not end when you leave the office; it continues to follow you home via emails and messages. Social media keeps you connected to your friends' and acquaintances' lives around the clock, giving the impression that you're always connected to social interactions. As the internet world competes for your attention, even your personal time, which should be a shelter, gets peppered with digital intrusions.

This has a far greater influence than it appears. It's not simply being distracted or having less time for yourself; it's how your mind begins to handle this continual connectivity. The way you prioritize work and conversations has changed subtly but significantly. Things like checking a notification might feel more urgent than they really are, overshadowing more significant, gratifying pursuits that demand more time and effort.

This 'always-on' mode can cause a condition of hypervigilance in which you are constantly awaiting the next ping, task, or update. It's a state that can keep your mind in a constant state of low-level stress, making relaxation and unwinding difficult. This can hurt your mental and emotional health over time, causing feelings of worry, restlessness, and overwhelm.

Social Media
Social media does, in fact, add a complicated layer to the fabric of your digital existence. Every time you click through your feed, you're faced with a flood of images and stories, each one more carefully managed and polished than the one before it. This isn't simply a random collection of posts; it's a carefully curated exhibition of the best moments, the highlights of other people's lives. Beautiful vacations, flawless outings, accomplishments, and celebrations - social media has become a highlight reel of life's best moments.

But herein lays the difficulty. When you scan through these photos, it's tempting to fall into the comparison trap. You see friends and acquaintances in seemingly wonderful situations and compare your life to this idealized online world. This comparison could be better. After all, with its ups and downs, your ordinary existence can't compete with these painstakingly chosen and edited peeks into someone else's life.

Continuous exposure to idealized representations of reality can lead to feelings of inadequacy and self-doubt. You may question why your life is less fascinating, spectacular, or gratifying than what you see on your screen. "Why isn't my house that clean? Why aren't my holidays as exotic as that? "Why doesn't my job appear to be as fulfilling?" These questions erode your contentment, feeding into a sense of inadequacy that can be difficult to escape.

Furthermore, this world of beautiful images might alter your expectations of what life should be like, not simply your view of it. It has the potential to set an unreasonable standard for happiness and success that is practically hard to attain. As a result, there is a constant sense of falling short, of failing to meet this created standard of perfection.

Because it operates subtly, this dynamic can be very insidious. You may not even realize how much these comparisons are hurting you. However, they can lead to chronic discontent and unease over time. This is where the influence of social media in promoting worry becomes clear. Constant exposure to idealized lives might make you feel as if you're always one step behind, chasing a version of life that doesn't fully exist.

Anonymity

Furthermore, with its veil of anonymity and physical distance, the digital world can frequently nurture a different type of social contact than you're used to in person. People may say things online that they would never say in person, resulting in harsher, more critical conversations. This phenomenon is not restricted to contact with strangers in public forums or on social media; it may even infiltrate conversations with acquaintances and friends.

When you dispute online, you lose the regular social cues and rules that govern face-to-face encounters. You can't see the other person's body language, hear their voice tone, or notice their immediate emotional reaction. This lack of contextual cues can lead to misconceptions and increase tensions, transforming a little personal disagreement into a major online conflict.

Negative internet remarks or criticisms might feel quite personal. It could be because these words, when typed down and put on a screen, can be read and re-read, reinforcing the pain each time. Ironically, the impersonal aspect of these exchanges makes them appear more direct and targeted, as if the words are speaking straight to you, lacking any human empathy or understanding.

Furthermore, online encounters frequently need more immediate resolution. Even if it's an agreement to disagree, a personal quarrel may end with a handshake or mutual understanding. However, there is frequently no apparent resolution to a debate online. After concluding the conversation, a bad comment might linger on your screen and in your mind. This unresolved tension can be a source of persistent concern and worry, leaving you contemplating the conversation, what was said, and what could have been stated differently.

This feature of digital communication can be especially stressful since it puts you in a state of limbo. Because online conflicts are open-ended, moving on or letting go of the bad feelings linked to the connection can be difficult. You may find yourself returning to the conversation on a mental and digital level, re-engaging with the disagreement and the feelings it evokes.

Space and Time

However, the digital age's most fundamental change is how you sense time and presence. With the entire world at your fingertips, there is an underlying demand to continuously do more, see more, and engage more. With their infinite streams of content and interaction, your digital devices can create a sense of limitless opportunity and possibilities. While exciting in its potential, this emotion can sometimes be overwhelming.

Your sense of time might become warped in our digitally saturated environment. Hours can pass while surfing social media, watching movies, or participating in online discussions. Because of the immediacy and accessibility of digital content, it is easy to lose track of time, creating the illusion that days are both boundless and strangely short. You have the uneasy impression that, despite your busy schedule, you could be more genuinely present and involved in meaningful things.

Furthermore, the digital era has reshaped the concept of presence. Being physically and cognitively engaged in your immediate environment and interactions used to be considered present. Presence is now divided into two realms: physical and digital. You can be physically present in a room while mentally being miles away, absorbed in a digital world. This duality can produce the paradoxical sensation of being linked and separated simultaneously.

While digital interactions provide a sense of connection, they frequently lack the depth and rewarding character of in-person encounters. A text message, an online comment, or a 'like' on social media can instantly span distances, yet they frequently fail to represent the full range of human emotions and nuances. The intricacies of a grin, the pleasure of an embrace, or confidence in a friend's voice are lost in digital translation. As a result, even though you are more connected than ever, you may yearn for more meaningful, deep, and fulfilling relationships.

Loneliness and unhappiness can result from this contradiction of connectedness and isolation. You can begin to doubt the quality of your connections and interactions. Are you actually engaging with others, or are you only scratching the surface of your digital acquaintances? This contradiction between your digital engagements' quantity and real-life friendships' quality can be stressful. It emphasizes the importance of striking a balance - finding methods to combine the ease and connection of the digital world with the depth and richness of real-life experiences and relationships.

STATISTICS AND TRENDS

It's useful to remember that you're part of a much wider picture while you go about your regular digital activities. The evidence on digital usage and its relationship to anxiety levels is both illuminating and depressing. These figures are more than just numbers; they are a reflection of a shared experience, a look into the lives of millions of people who, like you, are navigating the intricacies of the digital age.

Nielsen

Consider the findings of a comprehensive study conducted by Nielsen, a multinational measurement and data analytics organization. According to them, American adults now spend more than 11 hours daily engaged with various media forms. This figure reflects a huge increase over past years, not just a modest increase. It's a trend that indicates more than simply shifting individual habits; it represents a bigger shift in the digital media landscape.

This significant increase in media interaction has many facets. It includes listening to music, watching videos, perusing social media, reading articles, and streaming TV episodes and movies. Part of this increase can be ascribed to the spread of digital devices and the ease with which internet content can be accessed. Media consumption has become more accessible and routine as smartphones, tablets, and laptops have become more prevalent daily.

The changing landscape of digital media is also an important factor. A steady influx of new platforms and content types is competing for your attention. The development of streaming services such as Netflix, Hulu, and Amazon Prime has transformed how consumers watch TV series and movies, giving rise to the practice of binge-watching. Similarly, social media sites are constantly updating and adding features to increase user engagement, whether it's through Instagram stories, Facebook live videos, or TikTok's quick, bite-sized content.

Furthermore, the nature of media consumption has shifted. It is no longer a passive experience; it has evolved into a more interactive one. For example, social media isn't only for viewing other people's lives; it's also about sharing, commenting, and participating in content. This amount of connection might be fascinating, leading to you spending more time than you meant or thought.

This dramatic increase in media interaction has consequences for both mental and physical health. The more time spent with digital media, particularly in sedentary pursuits, the less time there is for physical activity and face-to-face relationships with family and friends. Long-term exposure to digital media, particularly social media, has been related to increased feelings of loneliness, anxiety, and depression in certain people.

The Nielsen report emphasizes an important facet of modern life: the necessity of awareness of our media consumption patterns. It is not only about the amount of time spent but also about the quality of that time. Maintaining a healthy, well-rounded lifestyle requires balancing digital media use with other key areas of life, such as physical activity, in-person social connections, and other offline hobbies. Understanding these patterns and their possible impact on your life is critical to achieving this balance.

Pew Research Center

Social media usage has increased dramatically, becoming a staple of many people's everyday lives. Platforms like Facebook, Instagram, and Twitter are no longer just socializing tools; they have evolved into complex hubs of activity. According to the Pew Research Center, around seven out of ten Americans use social media, with a sizable number visiting these sites at least once daily. This widespread adoption reflects a fundamental shift in how people communicate, gather information, and entertain themselves.

The role of social media has grown far beyond keeping in touch with friends and family. For many users, these sites have evolved into key news and information providers. People are increasingly turning to their social media feeds to keep up with current events, and these platforms are frequently the initial point of contact for breaking news stories. The speed with which information travels over these networks is unrivaled, making them effective tools for information distribution.

Furthermore, social media has evolved into an important arena for entertainment. These platforms provide various entertainment alternatives that cater to various interests and inclinations, from viral videos and memes to live streams and influencer content. The growth of short-form video content, as witnessed on platforms such as TikTok and Instagram Reels, has broadened the entertainment landscape even further, attracting the interest of younger people.

Social media platforms have evolved as important arenas for public discourse, social activism, and news and entertainment. They provide a space for people to express themselves, thoughts to be shared, and discussions to take place on various issues. Thanks to these platforms, users have been able to engage in societal concerns, mobilize for causes, and participate in civic discourse. The hashtag movements and online campaigns that acquire popularity on these platforms can potentially have real-world consequences and affect societal change.

However, the importance of social media in daily life has its challenges. The constant flow of information and the urge to keep connected digitally can be overwhelming. The ease with which a broad assortment of content may be accessed might lead to excessive screen time, potentially affecting mental well-being. Furthermore, the mix of news, opinion, and entertainment on these platforms can sometimes blur the lines between genuine information and misinformation, necessitating the development of consumers' critical thinking and media literacy skills.

In conclusion, the surge in social media usage indicates a greater shift in how people interact with the world around them. These platforms have grown commonplace, influencing how individuals acquire information, enjoy themselves, and engage in public conversation. Understanding the impact of social media on society and individual well-being remains a crucial area of consideration as it evolves.

Journal of Abnormal Psychology

While providing several benefits, this huge increase in digital participation has far-reaching consequences, notably for mental health and psychological well-being. Spending so much time online isn't just a passive activity; it actively impacts perceptions, habits, and mental state. For example, research published in the Journal of Abnormal Psychology highlights the possible repercussions of excessive screen usage.

The researchers discovered a link between the amount of time children and teenagers spend on screens and a decline in their psychological well-being. This relationship exemplifies a troubling tendency, particularly in light of the increasingly digitalized environment in which younger generations are growing up. The influence is multifaceted, affecting many facets of mental health.

One noticeable impact is an increase in concentration issues. Digital content's fast-paced, ever-changing nature can train young minds to demand constant stimulation. This expectation might make it difficult to retain focus and attention in less interesting or slower-paced contexts, such as schools or while reading. Digital media's continuous flipping of attention might hinder the development of sustained attention and concentration skills.

Furthermore, the study finds that heavy digital media users have worse self-esteem. This can be partly due to the social comparison that occurs frequently on social media sites. Young people are especially vulnerable to comparing their lives to the idealized versions portrayed by friends and influencers online, which can lead to feelings of inadequacy and self-worth. Because social media information is managed, it can set false benchmarks for personal accomplishment, attractiveness, and lifestyle against which people judge themselves.

Furthermore, the study links excessive screen usage to an increased risk of anxiety and despair. This link could be attributed to various variables, including altered sleep patterns caused by blue light exposure from screens, less physical activity, and less time spent engaging in face-to-face social contact. Cyberbullying, online harassment, and the pressure to maintain a certain online identity, in particular, can be a source of stress and anxiety on social media.

These findings send a clear message: the digital world, while useful and almost unavoidable in modern society, requires careful navigation, particularly by younger users. Balancing screen time with offline activities, encouraging face-to-face conversations, and cultivating a healthy connection with digital media are all important steps toward reducing these harmful effects. It is about establishing a digital world that promotes and enhances well-being rather than detracting from it. Understanding and managing the influence of digital technology on mental health is becoming increasingly crucial as it evolves, particularly for younger, more susceptible populations.

Journal of Preventive Medicine

A study published in the Journal of Preventive Medicine Reports sheds light on this, revealing a concerning link between screen time and adult mental health. According to this study, higher amounts of screen time were linked to an increased risk of moderate to severe depression among adults in the United States. This correlation emphasizes the reality that the implications of digital immersion affect people of all ages.

The reasons for this relationship are several. One key reason is the constant bombardment of information. Digital technology has ushered in an era of information overload, with news, updates, notifications, and messages constantly bombarding your displays. This never-ending stream can be mentally draining because it requires ongoing attention and cognitive processing. This additional layer of digital information can be stressful for adults who frequently juggle several tasks, increasing stress levels.

Another issue is the pressure to maintain social connections. While social media platforms provide chances for interaction and community building, they also foster an environment with an unwritten expectation to always be involved. This might emerge as a need to answer messages quickly, maintain an active social media presence, and keep up with the digital lives of friends, family, and even strangers. This pressure can be draining, leading to worry and inadequacy, especially if one's own life does not appear to match up to the managed lives of others shown online.

Furthermore, blurring the barriers between work and personal life exacerbates the problem. In an age when remote employment and internet contact are widespread, the lines that traditionally divided work and family life have become increasingly porous. Work-related emails and texts frequently intrude on personal time, extending the workweek beyond typical hours. This eroding of boundaries can lead to a sense of being always 'on call,' disrupting work-life balance, a critical component of mental well-being.

These factors, when combined, contribute to increased stress and anxiety in adults. While the digital landscape provides several benefits and conveniences, it also poses distinct difficulties to mental health. It is critical to recognize and address these issues. Setting clear boundaries for digital use, assigning time for unplugged activities, and being attentive to the quality and quantity of digital engagement can all contribute to this. As the digital world evolves, developing measures to protect mental health from the possible negative effects of prolonged screen time and digital immersion becomes increasingly vital.

The Results

But what does this mean for anxiety levels? Research indicates a strong correlation between increased digital usage and heightened anxiety, especially among younger demographics. For instance, a study found that high school students who spend more than 3 hours per day on social media are 60% more likely to report high levels of internalizing behaviors, which are indicative of anxiety and depression.

Moreover, the constant connectivity offered by smartphones and other digital devices has been linked to increased stress and difficulty disconnecting from work and social obligations. The blurring boundaries between work and personal life contribute to a sense of never truly being 'off duty,' which can heighten feelings of anxiety.

It's also worth noting that these trends have been accelerating. Over the past few years, there's been a noticeable uptick in digital consumption, partly fueled by societal shifts such as remote work and online education. This increased dependency on digital tools for everyday activities has made finding a balance and disconnect more challenging.

But remember, these statistics are not just cold facts; they represent real people, real experiences. They highlight a growing societal challenge – finding a healthy balance in our digital lives. Knowing that you're not alone in this can be comforting. It's a shared journey, and understanding these trends is the first step towards finding ways to manage your digital habits and, consequently, your anxiety levels. This empowering awareness leads you towards a more mindful and balanced relationship with the digital world.

CHAPTER 2: SOCIAL MEDIA AND ANXIETY

The Social Media Paradox

When you open your favorite social media app and scroll through the feed, you enter a world that connects and isolates you. This is the social media paradox, a phenomenon you most certainly encounter daily, sometimes without even realizing it.

On the one hand, social media connectivity is nothing short of revolutionary, a marvel that would have been difficult to envision just a few decades ago. Consider the sheer power and convenience at your disposal: with a few taps or clicks, you can cross massive geographical boundaries and connect with friends and family anywhere globally. This ability to stay linked crosses physical boundaries and time zones, making the world seem smaller and more connected.

Imagine celebrating a friend's accomplishment with a message that instantly transcends continents or sharing a photo that quickly sends smiles to faces thousands of miles away. Social media allows you to share life's significant and commonplace experiences with a network far beyond your immediate physical surroundings. Birthdays, graduations, new jobs, or a gorgeous sunset can now be shared and enjoyed collectively by individuals who are not physically present.

Furthermore, social media has the unrivaled potential to sustain and revitalize relationships that may have faded due to distance.

Friendships from high school, former colleagues, and distant relatives that may have faded into recollection can now be actively maintained. Despite the distance between you, you can engage with these people regularly, keeping up with their lives and continuing to share experiences.

On the other hand, a less visible but equally significant feature of social media is the sensation of isolation it can unknowingly engender. This separation is subtle and frequently goes unrecognized. While social media platforms allow you to contact many people, they frequently need more depth, complexity, and sincerity that come with face-to-face encounters. This disparity can result in a distinct type of loneliness, one that is felt in a virtual community.

Consider the nature of your internet relationships. You may have hundreds, if not thousands, of 'friends' or followers on social sites, but consider the quality of these connections. How many of them can provide actual emotional support? How many exchanges go beyond the surface-level 'likes' and comments? The reality is that the depth of online relationships frequently needs to catch up to the depth of in-person interactions. For all of its linking power, social media can leave you feeling isolated on a more intimate, emotional level.

Furthermore, the regulated nature of social media adds to this sense of isolation. Platforms are crammed with highly curated pictures of people's lives, frequently depicting an idealized, polished reality. It's a world where everyone looks to be on vacation all the time, where accomplishments are continuously lauded, and everyday life appears perfect. Constant exposure to other people's 'greatest moments' can lead to damaging comparisons. You may find yourself comparing your life to these supposedly flawless people's lives, wondering why your reality doesn't match what you see on your computer.

This comparison trap is really simple to slip into. You witness other people's accomplishments and happiness but not their hardships and monotonous times, which are unavoidably a part of their lives. This distorted image can lead to emotions of inadequacy, envy, and exclusion. You may begin to feel like a spectator in a life where you are not participating, as if everyone else is moving forward while lagging behind.

Within social media, the juxtaposition of connectivity and isolation produces a complicated and frequently problematic emotional landscape. On the surface, you appear to be more connected than ever. Your digital network spans continents and includes people from all stages of your life. However, amid this immense web of digital acquaintances, you may experience feelings of loneliness and isolation.

This distinct type of loneliness is caused not by being physically alone but by the nature of relationships and interactions in the digital environment. For its capacity to bring people together, social media can also encourage a sensation of being on the outside looking in. Constantly being exposed to finely edited glimpses of other people's lives might remove you from your own reality. As you scroll through feeds full of joyful celebrations, exotic adventures, and seemingly ideal daily moments, you may begin to feel more like an observer of life than an active player in your own story.

This sense of detachment from reality can be disconcerting. You're constantly assaulted with glimpses into other people's lives, yet these glances frequently lack the depth and authenticity of genuine human interactions. Conversations, shared experiences, and mutual understanding that emerge from in-person contacts are frequently diluted in the digital arena. As a result, the abundance of online contacts can appear superficial, leaving an emotional gap that the digital world cannot replace.

Furthermore, there might be a dramatic contrast between the brightness of the digital world and the realities of ordinary life.

Life is in continual high gear in the digital domain, with every moment a cause for celebration or display. In comparison, the daily routine, with its ups and downs, can appear mundane, if not dull. This mismatch might cause you to feel disconnected from your life, as if your reality is less than it should be.

Remember that your feelings in this digital dichotomy are valid and more prevalent than you may believe. Many struggle to reconcile social media's sense of connection with the feelings of isolation it may sometimes cause. The idea here is to strike a balance. It's about learning to appreciate the great features of these platforms—the connectivity, shared experiences, and sense of community—while remaining mindful of their propensity to foster feelings of isolation and inadequacy.

You must be deliberate in your social media use to achieve this balance. Begin by considering how you feel after spending time online. Do particular platforms or content uplift or drain you and make you feel inadequate? Use these insights to carefully curate your feed. Select accounts to follow and stuff to engage with that enriches your life and represents your values and interests. If you find that specific posts or interactions continually depress you, don't be afraid to mute, unfollow, or ban them. It is up to you to shape your digital space.

Consider setting limits on how much time you spend on social media. This could include designating specific parts of the day as ' social media-free or setting a daily time restriction for how much time you spend on these platforms. Apps and software that track your usage can help you stay within these limits. Limiting your screen time frees up time for other activities and relationships that can improve your well-being.

It is also critical to invest in your offline relationships and activities. Remember that the most significant and fulfilling connections are typically made in person. Spend time with family and friends, participate in hobbies, and attend community activities. These in-person encounters give richness and complexity that cannot be recreated online. They bring you back to the present moment and provide an antidote to the digital world.

It's also critical to develop a mindfulness and self-reflection practice. Check in with yourself and learn about your emotional reactions to digital encounters. This practice can help you become more aware of how social media impacts you and aid you in making decisions that benefit your mental and emotional health.

In essence, it's about developing a harmonious relationship with technology—one in which you control your digital interactions rather than being controlled by them. By striking this balance, you can reap the benefits of the digital world while limiting its drawbacks, resulting in a healthier, more fulfilled life.

COMPARISON AND SELF-ESTEEM

It's too easy to get caught up in comparison as you scroll through your social media feed. You see images of old classmates celebrating major accomplishments, friends on exotic holidays, or acquaintances living what appears to be the ideal family life. You compare your life to these pictures without even realizing it. This is the realm of comparison that social media so frequently welcomes you into, and it can significantly impact your self-esteem.

Remember that what you're seeing is only part of the picture. It's a highlight reel meticulously produced to highlight the best moments. However, recognizing this does not always keep thoughts of inadequacy at bay. You may wonder why your life isn't as fascinating, your achievements are smaller, or your happiness could be more obvious. It's a natural reaction but also a distorted one, comparing your behind-the-scenes to everyone else's highlight reel.

This continual comparison might erode your self-esteem. You may begin to value yourself depending on others' likes, comments, and perceived success rather than your own intrinsic worth. It's like a scale that never completely settles because the weight on the other side is a warped picture of truth.

But here's something to remember: these comparisons do not define your worth. Your value is intrinsic, not something to be evaluated against the seemingly perfect lives on a screen. It is about what you bring to the world, your traits and experiences, and how you influence people around you.

It may be necessary to take a step back occasionally to safeguard and nourish your self-esteem in this digital age. Unplug to reconnect with yourself. Participate in things that make you feel good about yourself and remind you of your talents, passions, and genuine connections. Surround yourself with individuals who know and appreciate the real you.

When you do utilize social media, attempt to do it with purpose. Instead of measuring your self-worth, use it to connect, inspire, and learn. Remember that you are more than your social media presence. You are a living, breathing story with chapters yet to be written, and that story is priceless in and of itself.

IMPACT ON IDENTITY

Have you ever considered how social media influences your identity as you navigate its convoluted web? Each post you make, and photo you publish helps to build an online persona that represents you to the rest of the world. This digital version of oneself can sometimes feel like a separate person, one that you carefully curate for an audience of friends, family, and strangers.

Consider how frequently you choose the best things of your life to share online. The bits that make it to your stream are the happy moments, the accomplishments, and the visually pleasing encounters. This selective sharing process might blur the lines between your genuine self and the one you display online over time. You may begin to feel pressure to live up to your digital persona, guaranteeing that your real life corresponds to the polished, perfected life you've portrayed on social media.

This pressure can be subtle, yet it can profoundly impact your feeling of identity and self-worth. You may make choices depending on how shareable they are or viewing your experiences through the prism of prospective social media content. This shift from living in the now to living for the 'gram' might cause a disconnect with your genuine self.

But remember that your identity is far richer and more complex than what can be expressed in a social media post. It's weaved from your experiences, relationships, ideals, and dreams, many of which never reach the screen. The quantity of likes, comments, or shares you receive does not determine your worth. It is based on the breadth of your experiences, your actions' generosity, and your quest's tenacity.

Finding strategies to stay loyal to your actual self in this digital age is critical. This could include taking breaks from social media, engaging in self-reflection, or simply reminding yourself that you are more than your online presence. Cultivate and treasure your offline life, where the moments are unfiltered, and the experiences are truly unique to you. Remember that your strongest qualities frequently do not require affirmation from a digital audience. They are the elements that distinguish you.

CHAPTER 3: INFORMATION OVERLOAD

The Era of Information

Have you noticed how continual access to information affects you in this information age, where the world's knowledge is just a click away? It's like standing beneath a digital waterfall, where news, updates, and notifications never cease. This never-ending flow of information may be both inspiring and overwhelming.

Consider your daily rhythm, interrupted not by the natural ebb and flow of life but by the constant ping of a new email, the buzz of a breaking news alert, or the chime of a social media update. Each message operates as a subtle tug on your attention, tugging it in different directions. It's as if you're in the middle of a web, with each thread begging your attention. This constant influx of information produces an undercurrent of urgency, a persistent sense that you must be constantly up to date with everything happening around you, both in your own life and the world at large.

This sensation of impending doom can be exhausting. While each warning or update may appear insignificant, it contributes to a broader tapestry of digital demand. It's like being in a room where everyone talks simultaneously; you might pick up on a few pieces here and there, but the overall impression is overpowering. This persistent state of vigilance can lead to digital tiredness in which your mind is constantly engaged, processing, and on.

This has a far greater influence than it appears. When your mind is continually inundated with fresh information, it has little opportunity to rest, reflect, or fully absorb one piece of information before the next arrives. It can feel like you're only scratching the surface of a sea of information, never diving deep enough to completely comprehend or appreciate any single component. This shallow connection with a large array of knowledge might leave you cognitively and emotionally disoriented.

Furthermore, the constant pressure on your time can make prioritizing what is genuinely important difficult. When everything feels important, it's difficult to tell what needs immediate attention and what can wait. You might react to the most recent notification rather than concentrate on more important chores or relationships.

This mental state of being constantly 'on' can be taxing. When your mind is constantly attentive and ready for the next information, it rarely has the chance to relax and recharge. Like a computer left operating without a halt, its efficiency gradually declines. Similarly, your brain begins to tire due to the constant barrage of information. This constant state of mental awareness is unsustainable in the long run and might hurt your overall health.

When your mind is constantly engaged, processing data streams, emails, social media updates, and news headlines, it is deprived of the necessary downtime. This constant mental activity can induce cognitive overload, in which the brain fails to receive and store new information because it is still dealing with old. It's like attempting to fill an already full cup. As a result, you may experience feelings of mental overwhelm, such as worry, irritation, and unease.

Furthermore, this persistent state of attention can impair your capacity to focus and concentrate. When you're used to quickly moving your attention from one notification to the next, having a fragmented attention span might become the norm, making it difficult to focus deeply on any task. This can develop into a sense of edginess over time, where you're physically present in a scenario but mentally dispersed, half-expecting another interruption or piece of information to come through.

The effects of cognitive tiredness are not restricted to your waking hours. It can even infiltrate your rest periods. With your mind racing or fixated on the knowledge you've consumed, you may find it difficult to unwind at the end of the day. A persistent sensation of mental unrest overshadows the time when you intend to relax and rejuvenate, making it difficult to fall or remain asleep and worsening feelings of exhaustion and anxiety the next day.

Acknowledging the importance of mental downtime is critical - intervals in which you allow your mind to wander, rest, and refresh. Setting aside certain periods of the day for digital detox, engaging in activities that promote relaxation, or simply giving yourself permission to take a break from the continual influx of information all contribute to this. You're improving your mental health and cognitive resilience, allowing you to return to your digital life refreshed and more ready to handle the flood of information.

You could notice the influence of this constant connectivity in your daily life, especially while you're supposed to be resting. Consider those times when you're lying in bed, the room is dark and silent, and you're ready to sleep soundly. Instead of falling asleep, your mind races, repeating the vast knowledge you've acquired over the day. The newest news headlines, the never-ending stream of social media updates, the emails you may have missed - all of these ideas spin about in your head, stopping you from finding the quiet required to fall asleep.

This battle isn't just for the night. Even when you should be taking a break, such as grabbing a cup of coffee in the morning or going for a short stroll, you may find yourself unconsciously reaching for your phone. There's almost a magnetic draw to check for updates, skim through feeds, and respond to messages. The desire to be constantly connected and 'in the know' can be overwhelming. You feel that by keeping up with this never-ending flood of information, you'll be able to get ahead of it, gaining control over the overwhelming tide of data.

On the other hand, this persistent interaction can have the opposite impact, further entrenching the feeling of being overwhelmed. Instead of providing control, it fosters a loop in which your mind is constantly engaged, constantly busy, and never completely at rest. The irony is that your efforts to stay on top of things make you feel more buried, trapped in an endless cycle of consume-and-react that allows little room for relaxation or mental comfort.

It is critical to recognize these patterns and their impact on your well-being. Taking purposeful breaks from digital connectedness – moments when you choose to disengage and allow your mind the space it needs to unwind – can be quite beneficial. These pauses don't have to be extensive; even brief intervals can help reset your mind, allowing you to return to your digital life with a fresh perspective and a calmer frame of mind. Remember, in a world that values continual connectivity, unplugging, being present at the moment, and allowing oneself the space to be might be the most rebellious and healing thing you can do.

RECOGNIZING OVERLOAD SYMPTOMS

As you go about your day, engaged in a world of digital information, it's critical to detect the warning signs that you're becoming overwhelmed. These symptoms may be minor initially, gradually worsening until they become more visible and interfere with your regular life.

Mental Fatigue

One of the first indicators you may detect in this digital age is a persistent sense of mental exhaustion that persists even after a restful night's sleep. It's as if your brain is always processing and storing the onslaught of information you've collected during the day. This constant cerebral activity can be exhausting, leaving you feeling depleted and exhausted but unsure why, especially if you've been physically inactive.

This mental tiredness presents itself in a variety of subtle but significant ways. For example, you may discover that your ability to concentrate on tasks is no longer what it was. Tasks that appeared simple before now take greater effort and concentration. Your mind may wander more frequently, making staying focused on your work or conversing with people difficult. This is a frequent feeling in a world where our attention is continuously divided among numerous information streams.

You may also notice an increase in forgetfulness. At first, it could be as simple as misplacing your keys, forgetting appointments, or needing help recalling names and facts. This isn't necessarily a sign of a deeper cognitive problem but rather that your brain is overloaded with information. When your mental capacity is constantly consumed by the processing of digital stuff, it leaves less room for other cognitive tasks like short-term memory and attention to detail.

This mental tiredness can also emerge as a reduced ability to think creatively and solve problems. Overwhelmed by the volume of processed information, the brain may struggle to generate new ideas or solutions, affecting your creativity and productivity.

Recognizing these indicators of mental tiredness is critical for taking the initial steps toward coping with digital information overload. It's your mind telling you that it needs a break from the steady inflow of information. Recognizing this allows you to begin implementing techniques to provide your brain with the rest it needs, whether through digital detox, mindful practices, or just scheduling time for relaxation and activities that engage you in the physical world. Remember that mental health is just as important as physical health, and preserving it in this digital age is critical for living a balanced and fulfilled life.

Irritability

Another symptom you may have in this age of continual digital connectivity is irritability or restlessness. It's as if your regular patience and tolerance levels have been reduced. Small inconveniences you would normally dismiss may now elicit a larger, more immediate emotion. It could be a sluggish internet connection, a slight mistake in an email, or even common noises that have become more annoying than usual. These sensations of anger might be unexpected and upsetting, especially if you are generally relatively calm.

This restlessness can also be characterized by difficulty in relaxing or settling into any activity for an extended amount of time. You may find yourself continuously switching things, unable to focus on one thing, or feeling compelled to check your phone even when there is no pressing need. It's as if your mind is continually alert, waiting for the next notification or batch of information to digest.

This constant state of attention can be mentally and emotionally taxing. It indicates that your mind is overburdened, flooded with digital stimulus, and desperately needs a break. With its never-ending streams of information and stimulus, the digital world can keep your brain on high alert, making it difficult to unwind and rest.

Recognizing these emotions of irritation and restlessness as indications of information overload is critical. They are signs that it is time to take a step back and allow your mind some much-needed relaxation. Setting aside particular times to check emails and social media, as well as participating in relaxing activities such as reading a book, going for a walk, or practicing mindfulness and meditation, can all help. It is about carving out time in your day when you are not assaulted with digital stimuli, allowing your mind to calm and heal. In a digitally saturated environment, doing these actions can help restore your regular levels of patience and serenity and boost your general sense of well-being.

Mood

You may also notice changes in your mood that appear unexplainable at first. Anxiety or a persistent sadness that appears out of nowhere could be attributed to digital information overload. In today's environment, when you're constantly bombarded with news and updates, it's not uncommon for these digital inputs to impact your emotional state.

Consider the nature of much of the news you see online. It frequently focuses on negative or upsetting occurrences, such as natural disasters, political conflicts, and public health problems. While it is crucial to keep informed, repeated exposure to distressing stories can significantly influence your emotional well-being. You may notice that your mood begins to mimic the tone of the news you consume, resulting in emotions of melancholy, anxiety, or overall unease.

This emotional response can be slow and subtle. You may not instantly associate your feelings of worry or depression with your digital activities. It's like a steady stream of negativity seeping into your consciousness, influencing your outlook and mood. Over time, this might build to a state of emotional tiredness in which you feel depleted and down with no evident cause.

The psychological cost of this is not to be ignored. It can impact your interactions with people, productivity, and general quality of life. You may become more pessimistic, less driven, or cynical, which might worsen feelings of melancholy or worry.

Recognizing the link between your internet intake and mood is an important first step in reducing its impact. It may include limiting your exposure to news media, particularly ones that focus on bad stories. It may also entail deliberately seeking out good and uplifting content to counteract the negativity. Furthermore, engaging in activities that enhance emotional well-being, such as exercise, spending time in nature, or interacting with loved ones, can help offset digital overload's impacts.

Physical
Physical symptoms are as striking as mental and emotional signs when it comes to being overwhelmed by digital information. Spending long periods in front of a screen can cause a variety of bodily discomforts, some of which you may not immediately attribute to your digital habits.

Headaches are a typical symptom, often caused by gazing at a screen for an extended period. This could be related to eye strain, particularly if you're reading small print or staring at a bright screen without taking regular breaks. Screen blue light can also contribute to headaches by disrupting sleep-wake cycles and straining your eyes.

Another symptom is eye strain. After prolonged computer, tablet, or smartphone use, your eyes may become dry, itchy, or weary. This is caused by the screen's light and the reduced frequency of blinking when focusing on digital information, which can induce eye dryness and irritation.

Then there's the stiffness in your neck and shoulders, a physical reflection of the stress and strain that comes with continual connectedness. Poor posture while using devices can increase this, resulting in muscle stiffness and discomfort. This can progress to chronic pain over time, limiting not just your comfort but also your ability to relax and unwind.

Excessive screen time can also substantially alter your sleep patterns. You may have difficulty falling asleep since the mental stimulus from screen use keeps your brain engaged. Alternatively, you may wake up repeatedly during the night while your mind continues to absorb the information from the day. Screen blue light can also interfere with the generation of melatonin, the hormone that regulates sleep, disturbing your sleep cycle even further.

These bodily signs are your body's way of saying it's time to take a break and reconsider your digital habits. Regular screen breaks, excellent posture, and screen-free time before bed can help reduce these symptoms.

STRATEGIES FOR MANAGING DIGITAL OVERLOAD

Effectively managing digital overload is critical in our increasingly connected environment, and it entails more than just taking breaks from screens. It would be best to incorporate many tactics into your daily routine to reduce the impact of constant digital involvement. This isn't about hating technology or digital connectedness, providing enormous benefits and conveniences. It's about developing a more balanced relationship with these tools, ensuring they assist you rather than overwhelm you.

Incorporating these tactics involves intentional effort and, in some cases, a shift in habits. It's about knowing how, when, and why you use digital gadgets and recognizing the warning signs when they negatively affect your wellbeing. By proactively limiting your digital intake, you may reduce stress, boost focus, and improve your general quality of life.

Each plan should be adapted to your specific lifestyle and needs. What works for one person may not work for another, so it's crucial to experiment to find out what works best for you in managing your digital life. The idea is to gain control over your digital interactions, making your online time more thoughtful and less reactive.

Setting Defined Digital Boundaries: Setting specific periods for reading emails, social media, and news can be extremely beneficial in dealing with digital overload. You build an organized approach to your digital involvement by allocating specific periods for these activities. This can help alleviate the sensation of being continually drawn into the digital world. For example, avoiding screens for the first hour after waking up can provide you a serene start to the day, giving you time to focus on your daily routine without interruptions. Similarly, avoiding screens in the last hour before bed will help your mind unwind and prepare for sleep, resulting in better sleep quality. These limitations regulate your digital life and allow you to devote more time to other important tasks or relaxation.

Implementing Screen-Free Periods: Making certain periods of the day or days of the week screen-free can significantly impact your wellbeing. This may imply enforcing a 'no screens' policy during meals, freeing time for more meaningful talks with family. Alternatively, you may designate one day per week as a digital detox day, devoting it to hobbies or activities you enjoy doing away from the computer. During these screen-free periods, you can engage in activities such as reading a book, experiencing nature, or simply interacting with friends and family. These digital gadget breaks help you to reconnect with the environment around you, cultivating a sense of presence and awareness.

Attentive Scrolling: Attention to how and why you use your digital devices can help you reduce unnecessary screen time. Pause momentarily before unlocking your phone or opening your laptop to ponder your goal. Are you about to do something constructive or required, or are you just searching for something to do to pass the time? Mindful scrolling entails becoming aware of your digital behaviors and selecting online activities that are meaningful and give worth to your life. Rather than passively browsing your social media feeds, you may consume something that informs or inspires you. You can become more intentional in your digital interactions by engaging in mindful scrolling, resulting in a more balanced and rewarding online experience.

Mindful Technology usage: Mindful technology utilizes the different features and settings available on your digital devices to minimize disruptions and better manage your online time. Using the 'Do Not Disturb' mode while at Work or with family can help you stay focused and present by decreasing the continual flood of alerts. Setting app limits or utilizing screen time tracking features can also be advantageous. These programs enable you to track and regulate how much time you spend on individual apps, pushing you to be more deliberate with your screen time. Customizing notification settings to receive alerts only from necessary apps or contacts can dramatically reduce the frequency of digital disruptions, allowing you to interact with technology on your terms rather than being at its continual beck and call.

Digital Detox Sessions: Scheduling digital detox sessions regularly can be a great method to reset your mind and minimize your reliance on digital devices. This might promise to turn off all digital gadgets for a specific time, such as a day or a weekend. You give yourself permission to walk away from the digital world at this time, enabling your mind to relax and replenish. When you return to the digital realm, these breaks can give you a new perspective, leading to better creativity and productivity. Digital detox sessions also urge you to reconnect with the actual world and participate in activities that you may have ignored due to excessive screen usage.

Prioritizing Physical Activity: Participating in physical activity is an excellent method to naturally disconnect from digital gadgets and boost your general wellbeing. Walking, yoga, and team sports not only urge you to leave your electronics at home, but they also boost physical health and mental clarity. These exercises serve a dual purpose: they provide a break from screens while contributing to physical fitness. Regular physical activity can also boost mood, reduce stress and anxiety, and improve sleep quality, offsetting some negative impacts of excessive screen time. By including physical activities into your routine, you can balance your digital and physical lives well.

Creating a Relaxing Bedtime Habit: Creating a screen-free bedtime habit is critical for increasing sleep quality. Screen blue light can interfere with your body's normal production of melatonin, the hormone that governs sleep, making it difficult to fall asleep. Instead of concluding your day with digital gadgets, think about activities that indicate to your body that it's time to unwind. Reading a book, for example, not only relaxes but also stimulates your intellect in a different, more peaceful way than screen-based media. Meditation or light stretching activities can also help prepare your body and mind for sleep. These activities can serve as cues to aid in the shift into a restful state, resulting in deeper and more restorative sleep.

Organizing Your Digital Environment: Just as cleaning up your physical living environment can relieve stress and create a sense of serenity, organizing your digital space can do the same. Decluttering your digital environments regularly can help you manage your online life more successfully. Begin with your email inbox; unsubscribe from unneeded mailing lists and categorize key emails in folders. Apply the same logic to your social media feeds: unfollow or mute accounts that offer no value to your life or negatively impact your mood. Organize your phone apps, retaining only those you use regularly and removing or archiving the rest. A decluttered digital area can result in a more focused and less stressful digital experience in which you are not continually bombarded with irrelevant information.

Engaging in 'Deep Work' Sessions: In a world full of digital distractions, making time for focused, uninterrupted Work is crucial. Deep Work sessions entail devoting time to focusing on a single work or project without interruptions. These are all examples of turning off notifications, shutting extraneous internet tabs, and giving your whole focus to the subject at hand. These sessions can help you increase your concentration and productivity, allowing you to complete more Work in less time. Deep Work makes you more effective and gives you a sense of accomplishment and satisfaction since you can completely engage with and complete your duties without being distracted by digital distractions.

Seeking Real-Society Connections: In a digitally dominated society, it is critical to make a concerted effort to establish face-to-face interactions and experiences. While digital conversations can keep you linked across long distances, they frequently lack in-person relationships' depth and emotional richness. Spend time with family and friends, engage in conversations, and participate in group activities. These in-person relationships can create a sense of warmth, belonging, and fulfillment that internet connections cannot. Face-to-face encounters also allow for a more nuanced interchange of emotions and expressions, which promotes deeper understanding and stronger ties. Make a point of participating in social activities that promote human interaction regularly, such as joining clubs, attending community events, or simply having coffee with a buddy. These ties keep you grounded in the actual world and remind you of the pleasures and advantages of human interaction.

Gratitude & Mindfulness Practices: Incorporating mindfulness and gratitude into your daily routine can significantly impact your mental well-being and outlook. Mindfulness enables you to be present in the moment, which reduces stress and promotes tranquility. Simple activities such as mindful breathing, mindful eating, or observing your thoughts without judgment can help focus your mind and mitigate the effects of digital overload. Similarly, practicing gratitude can help redirect your attention away from what's missing or overwhelming in your digital life and toward the abundance and positivity in your real life. Keeping a gratitude notebook or simply thinking about a few things you're grateful for every day can boost your attitude and outlook and provide a more balanced perspective on your daily life.

Educating Yourself on Digital Wellness: In this day and age of rapid technological innovation, it is critical to keep knowledgeable about digital wellness and the impact of technology on mental health. Learn about the pros and pitfalls of digital consumption and how it can affect your mental health. Understanding the fundamentals of digital wellness can help you make educated decisions regarding your digital habits. Look for materials, attend workshops, or join online communities that explore digital wellbeing. The more you understand how technology impacts your mind and body, the more prepared you will be to manage your digital life in a way that promotes your general wellbeing. Knowledge in this area can also assist you in setting a good example for others and raising awareness about the necessity of maintaining a healthy balance with technology.

CHAPTER 4: DIGITAL COMMUNICATION AND MISCOMMUNICATION

The Impact of Digital Communication

As you go about your day, assess how much of your communication is via texting, emails, and instant chatting. Have these digital ways of communication become embedded in your everyday routine? While they provide tremendous convenience and fast communication, you should consider how they may be affecting your anxiety levels.

Texting and instant messaging have really altered the communication scene, haven't they? Because of their immediacy and convenience, they imply an unstated expectation of prompt responses. Consider how many times you have received an SMS or a message. Do you have a sudden sense of urgency and need to reply immediately? It's almost reflexive to pause whatever you're doing to respond. This expectation, whether self-inflicted or imposed by others, can quietly create in you a sense of perpetual attention.

This demand to be immediately responsive might become a never-ending loop. You send a message and then keep checking your phone for a response. Alternatively, if you receive a message, you may abandon your current task to react, no matter how urgent. This can cause you to lose focus, fragment your time, and feel more anxious and stressed. It's as if you're always 'on call,' psychologically prepared to act.

This constant state of alertness can be mentally and emotionally taxing. It isn't easy to fully participate in the current moment or immerse yourself in any task when your attention is continually divided. It can also cause a fear of missing out or disappointing someone if you don't answer immediately. This continual awareness and pressure to be constantly ready might lead to feelings of burnout over time.

It is critical to note that this sensation of urgency is frequently produced by oneself and is not always essential. Most SMS and messages can wait; finishing your work before answering is fine. Setting boundaries around digital communication, such as setting times to check and respond to messages, might help relieve some of this stress.

Then, there's the problem of digital communication tone, which may need to be easier to interpret. Messages can become a puzzle without the visual indications of facial expressions, aural cues of tone of voice, or context offered by body language. Have you ever received a text or email perplexed by its tone? Perhaps you read a message that looked abrupt or curt, leading you to think whether the sender was upset or furious with you, even if that wasn't their intention.

In the digital era, ambiguity is a typical source of anxiety. A simple sentence can be construed in various ways since it needs the nuances of spoken speech. A simple "okay" in a text, for example, could be interpreted as approval, indifference, or even displeasure, depending on how you perceive it. Similarly, an email that skips the typical pleasantries and goes right to the point can be impersonal or chilly, even if the sender was merely trying to be brief.

This type of misunderstanding might cause undue anxiety and tension. You may find yourself revisiting communications to uncover the true meaning behind the words. In other circumstances, you may need to compose many copies of a response to effectively convey your tone, adding stress and time to what should be straightforward communication.

Because of the need for more clarity in digital communication, an additional degree of emotional interpretation is typically required, which can be intellectually exhausting. To address this, some people use emojis or clearly declare their feelings in their texts to offer context. However, acknowledging the limitations of digital communication and giving people the benefit of the doubt may be the best way. Consider a follow-up call or face-to-face contact for clarification if a message is unclear or appears odd.

Emails, particularly those relating to work, can certainly contribute to your anxiousness. Email is frequently the primary form of contact in the business world, and with it comes an unending stream that can feel overwhelming. Each email in your inbox, whether a new assignment, a request for information, or an update on a current project, demands your attention and action. It's like a never-ending to-do list that continues renewing itself no matter how hard you try to keep up.

The pressure to keep an empty inbox can be enormous. There is often an expectation, whether self-inflicted or imposed by your company culture, to react promptly to every email. This might result in a continual state of vigilance, where you're constantly checking for new messages, afraid about missing anything crucial or not responding quickly enough. This urge to be always responsive can break your focus on other tasks, fragment your workday, and add to a sense of being perpetually behind.

Furthermore, the sheer volume of communications might be intimidating. Opening your inbox and seeing a slew of unread messages can set off a stress response. Prioritizing, responding to, and sorting these emails can be time-consuming and mentally demanding. The diversity of the content within these emails necessitates frequent shifting of your focus and priorities.

Setting reasonable expectations and boundaries is essential for dealing with email-related stress. This may imply setting aside times during the day to check and respond to emails rather than continually watching your inbox. It may also entail employing organizational tools such as filters, folders, and labels to make your inbox more manageable.

Remember that while digital communication is a necessary element of modern life, managing it in a way that does not increase your worry is critical. This could include scheduling times to check your messages, allowing yourself to not answer immediately, or clarifying unclear conversations with a quick phone call. It's all about striking a balance that allows you to profit from these technologies without disrupting your peace of mind.

MISINTERPRETATIONS AND CONFLICTS

As you negotiate the complex world of digital communication, keep in mind the impact that misinterpretations and disagreements can have in raising your anxiety levels. Without face-to-face contact, where nuances of tone, expression, and body language are obvious, digital chats can occasionally lead to misunderstandings.

Assume you're sitting in front of your phone or computer, having just sent a message or an email. The tone and intent of your statements are clear in your thoughts. When the message reaches the other person, it is filtered by their views, emotions, and circumstances. This is where digital misunderstandings occur.

When there is a misunderstanding between what you intended to say and how the recipient understands it, digital miscommunication happens. You need to have the luxury of rapid response or the capacity to use body language or tone of voice to clarify your intent in digital conversations. While typed, a simple phrase that was innocent or even hilarious while uttered can come across as harsh or rude.

Consider how often you've gotten a text or email and been unsure of the sender's genuine thoughts or intentions. Was their quick response a sign of irritation, or were they simply in a hurry? Did the lack of emojis or exclamation points indicate that something was wrong? These are textbook illustrations of how readily digital communication may be misunderstood.

Miscommunication in the digital arena can frequently result in a chain reaction of emotional responses. When you're on the receiving or sending end of a message with unclear intent, it can cause confusion and worry. Consider sending a message and then waiting for a response, with each passing minute increasing your anxiety. Was there a misunderstanding? Did you mention something incorrectly? This interval of waiting, common in digital communication, can feel interminable as your imagination races through possible situations and interpretations.

Similarly, if you receive an ambiguous or unexpected message, you may be in a loop of overthinking. You re-read the message, scrutinizing each word and punctuation mark to decipher the true meaning. Overanalyzing can be extremely taxing because you're trying to fill in the spaces and discern nuances that may or may not exist.

If there is a delay in responding, the worry can increase. Feedback is frequently immediate in face-to-face talks, and misunderstandings can be immediately clarified. However, a lack of fast response in digital communication can lead to a buildup of stress. You may begin to form storylines in your head, speculating on the other person's sentiments or reactions, frequently making unfavorable assumptions.

This sense of ambiguity can occasionally lead to conflict, especially if misconceptions are handled slowly. A curt or disinterested message can be the spark that ignites a greater misunderstanding. Furthermore, the impersonal aspect of Internet communication can often encourage people to say things they would not say in person, increasing the possibility of confrontation.

It's crucial to remember that many signs we rely on in real conversations are missing in digital communication. Recognizing this can help reduce the anxiety caused by misinterpretations.

When in doubt, seeking clarification in a non-aggressive manner can be beneficial. A follow-up message, a phone call, or even an in-person meeting might help clear up misconceptions before they become larger disputes.

Remember that seeking connection and understanding in your encounters is natural. Being patient, careful, and explicit in your communication will help lessen the tension that emerges from digital miscommunications in the digital world, where things can sometimes be lost in translation.

STRATEGIES FOR CLARITY AND UNDERSTANDING

It is critical to arm yourself with tactics that promote clarity and understanding when navigating the convoluted maze of digital communication. Understanding how to deliver your message clearly when engaging in online interactions, whether via emails, texts, or social media, may make a major difference in how it is received and interpreted.

Language
To begin, when engaging in digital communication, paying close attention to the language you use is critical. Each word in a text or email is more important than you imagine. Without vocal clues, your choice of words becomes the major tool for communicating your emotions, intentions, and thoughts. Choose words that clearly and accurately express your meaning to reduce the chance of misinterpretation.

For example, an answer as basic as "okay" can be ambiguous in a world of short texts and brief emails. Without more context, it can be difficult to tell whether you're reluctantly agreeing, confirming understanding, or expressing disinterest. A more descriptive remark, on the other hand, can provide much-needed clarity. "Okay, I understand and will get back to you by tomorrow," or "Okay, that sounds great!" are unambiguous indicators of your mood and intent.

When writing a message, read it from the recipient's point of view. Are there any words or phrases that could be interpreted incorrectly? Could the tone be overly formal, nonchalant, or even dismissive? Maintaining a balance between being concise and polite is essential in professional settings. Mirroring the vocabulary and tone of the other person might help you match their communication style in more personal discussions.

Tone

The tone is crucial in how your digital messages are perceived. It's very easy for the tone of your messages to be misread without the nuances of vocal inflection and intonation that express so much in face-to-face talks. This is where emoticons and punctuation come into play as valuable tools for expressing what words alone may not adequately represent.

Consider using emojis; these small symbols can bring a whole new dimension of emotional content to your message. A smiley face at the end of a sentence can make a cold statement seem nicer and more welcoming. Emojis can indicate comedy, lighten the tone, or show you speaking pleasantly. Punctuation marks also play an important function. For example, an exclamation mark might show excitement or enthusiasm, making your message appear more dynamic and uplifting.

However, it is critical to keep your audience and the context of your message in mind. While emoticons and humorous punctuation are ideal for casual texts or communications with close coworkers, they are not necessarily appropriate in more official or business settings. For example, it's best to use a more traditional and formal tone in a business email. Excessive use of emojis or exclamation points in such situations may come out as unprofessional or overly casual.

It all comes down to finding the perfect balance and recognizing the conventions of your particular communication setting. Tone can still be conveyed professionally through word choice and sentence construction. For example, phrases like "I'm thrilled to announce..." or "I'm looking forward to..." can indicate excitement without emojis or exclamation marks.

Boundaries

Setting clear boundaries and expectations is an excellent method to prevent and manage potential disputes when navigating the complexities of digital communication. This entails being clear and transparent about how and when you prefer to communicate. By doing so, you develop a mutual understanding that can assist you and your communication partners in managing expectations and lessen worry.

For example, you focus on deep work during particular hours and limit email checks to specific periods. In that case, it's useful to explain this to your coworkers. You might set up an automatic email response to notify senders of your email checking schedule, or you could alert your colleagues during meetings. This way, people know you are paying attention to their messages and will answer promptly. Such openness can help avoid misunderstandings regarding delayed responses and alleviate the pressure you may feel to continually check and react to emails.

Similarly, suppose you're in charge of a team. In that case, setting clear criteria for preferred communication methods and reaction times is a good idea. For example, determining whether to utilize email vs. instant messaging can expedite communication and create clear expectations. You may determine that emails are for non-urgent, detailed communication, whereas instant messaging is for immediate, urgent demands.

Setting boundaries in personal communication is equally important. If you discover that regular notifications from social media or messaging applications are becoming too much for you, inform your friends and family that you are attempting to reduce your screen usage for mental health reasons. Most people will understand and appreciate your decision, which can help relieve the stress of feeling like you must always be present.

Clarification

If you find yourself in a scenario of misinterpretation in your digital connections, addressing it honestly and as soon as possible might be critical in preventing additional misunderstanding. If left unresolved, miscommunication can cause unnecessary uncertainty, upset feelings, or even conflict. Thus, they must be addressed.

When you suspect that a message you sent was misunderstood, or when you get a message that leaves you feeling unclear or confused, asking for an explanation might help clarify the air. You may begin with a simple follow-up message that provides additional clarification or requests more information. By way of example, you might say, "I just wanted to clarify my previous message to make sure it was understood as I intended," or just, "I'm not sure I fully understand your last message. Could you please elaborate a bit more?"

Digital communication issues are frequently caused by a need for more nuance that is present in face-to-face encounters. When there is a significant miscommunication or the topic is sensitive, elevating the conversation to a more direct communication style might be beneficial. A phone conference, video chat, or in-person meeting allows for a more lively exchange. It enables tone of voice, facial expressions, and immediate feedback to deliver and comprehend messages more correctly.

It is beneficial to approach such conversations with openness and a willingness to comprehend the other person's point of view. The purpose is to clear up the confusion, not to prove a point or assign blame. You may address the issue more successfully and deepen the relationship by expressing your intentions clearly and listening to the other person's point of view.

Remember that good digital communication is about more than just sending information; it's about preserving relationships and understanding in a world where digital exchanges are increasingly supplementing face-to-face conversations. By implementing these tactics, you can navigate the digital communication maze more comfortably and confidently, resulting in more gratifying and less stressful online relationships.

CHAPTER 5: THE WORK-HOME BLUR

Remote Work and Digital Connectivity

You may know the difficulties of managing your professional and personal lives as you negotiate the world of remote work and internet connectivity. The barriers between business and personal time can blur in this digital age, where your house has become your office, generating unique issues.

As you adjust to the complications of remote work and digital connectivity, you may become more aware of the complexity of balancing your professional and personal lives in this digital age, where the lines between home and business blur, a new set of obstacles emerges, making balancing more difficult than ever.

Your home, which was once a refuge from the noise and bustle of the office, has now become your workspace. While this transition provides unparalleled flexibility, it also introduces a new challenge: blurring the barriers between your job and personal lives. The exact things that allow you to work remotely - your laptop and your smartphone – often bind you to your employment in ways that can be difficult to break free from. Because of this ongoing contact, it can be difficult to shut off from work mode.

Think about how this overlap affects your daily activities. Your living room or kitchen table, where you have set up your laptop, now serves as an area for family connection and personal rest. When you're in the same physical place, it might not be easy to psychologically move from a conference call to family time. Similarly, the lack of a physical commute, which traditionally marked the start and end of the workday, may lead to you working longer hours, unknowingly allowing work to infiltrate into time previously dedicated to personal pursuits or rest.

This new manner of working may muddy the lines of availability. You may feel pressured to reply to professional messages outside of typical working hours if you are expected to be reachable at all times. There's a notion that because your office is in your home, you're always at work, which makes it difficult to distinguish when you're at work' and when you're not.

The freedom that remote work provides can be a double-edged sword. On the one hand, it gives you the flexibility to schedule your job around your life rather than the other way around. You can begin your day on your own schedule, take breaks as needed, and work in the most comfortable area. This autonomy can be extremely liberating, allowing you to personalize your work life to your specific requirements and circumstances.

This same adaptability, however, can quietly transform into a sense of being constantly 'on call.' The digital tools that allow you to work from anywhere — your laptop, smartphone, or tablet – also bind you to your workplace in ways that can be difficult to break free from. There is frequently an unspoken expectation that you should be willing to do so because you have the flexibility to work whenever and wherever you choose. This can result in situations where you're checking and replying to business emails late at night or devoting time on weekends to work duties - times that were traditionally reserved for personal life, relaxation, and detachment from work.

The blurring of the lines between work and leisure time might be subtle. At first, you might not even realize it is happening. A simple email check in the evening can grow into an hour's worth of labor; a quick peek at a project on a Saturday can take up your entire afternoon. Work can gradually intrude on your personal time, making it difficult to find when you need to think about work-related responsibilities.

The difficulty in completely disconnecting is the main issue here. When your house serves as your office, the physical indicators that indicate the conclusion of the workday are absent. There is no getting out of the office, no commuting home to unwind. Your work is always only a few steps away, making it tempting to 'just do a little more' or ' stay on top of things.' This might create a pattern in which you feel obligated to be present and productive at all times, which can be psychologically and emotionally tiring over time.

In a remote working setting, merging work and home life can sometimes elicit complicated emotions, such as guilt or inadequacy. It might not be easy to shed the sense that you should always be doing more work when your house doubles as your office. You may feel bad for leaving your desk even after a hard day's work. It's as if living close to your workplace acts as a continual reminder of the never-ending tasks and responsibilities, making it difficult to actually feel 'off duty.'

On the other hand, devoting time to your career occasionally leads to sentiments of ignoring your personal life or family duties. You may be physically there at home when working on a project or attending multiple virtual meetings, but your head is elsewhere. This might cause guilt, especially if you cannot engage in family activities or handle personal problems during typical 'home hours.' You may find yourself divided between the responsibilities of your career and the necessities of your personal life, attempting to meet both yet feeling as if you are falling short in either.

This careful balancing act is a common difficulty in remote work. Trying to meet the responsibilities of your career while also taking care of yourself and your loved ones is a difficult endeavor.

Setting boundaries and managing your time successfully takes conscious effort.

Being aware of your need for personal time and space is critical in this day of digital connection, where work may follow you everywhere. It is about allowing yourself to detach, regenerate, and be present in your life outside of work. Balancing distant work and personal life is a continuous process that necessitates self-awareness and proactive effort to ensure that both elements of your life receive the time and care they need.

SETTING BOUNDARIES

Setting limits becomes increasingly necessary as you adapt to the digital environment, whether for job or personal reasons. Consider your daily interactions with digital gadgets like your phone, laptop, or tablet. They are portals to a never-ending stream of information, communication, and, at times, distraction. Isn't becoming lost in this digital jungle without defined boundaries easy? The idea is to set boundaries that allow you to reap technology's benefits while protecting your health.

When setting limits in your digital life, it's critical to think of them as tools that will help you develop a healthy and satisfying existence. These limits are strong statements about your priorities and ideals. They symbolize your dedication to protecting your time and energy and investing it in ways that will benefit your life.

By setting clear limitations on your digital involvement, you're effectively creating a zone where your personal needs and well-being are emphasized. It's like painting a line that separates your digital life from your personal life. This distinction is critical in a society where the boundaries between work, leisure, and personal space are becoming increasingly blurred.

Setting these boundaries also communicates to people around you - your colleagues, friends, and family - what you value and how you manage your time. It's a saying that you appreciate your work and contacts but also value your well-being and the quality of your offline life. This can assist in managing expectations and developing mutual respect for each other's time and space.

Setting limits is also an act of self-compassion. Knowing that to perform well, you must take time to unplug, unwind, and engage in activities that offer you joy and relaxation. Spending uninterrupted time with loved ones, pursuing a pastime, or simply enjoying moments of solitude are all important for your mental and emotional wellness.

Setting boundaries is also about reclaiming control in a world where digital technology can easily devour large quantities of your time. It's about making deliberate choices about how you interact with technology, ensuring that it improves rather than degrades the quality of your life.

Specific Times

Setting aside time to read emails and social media is an excellent way to handle digital overload. It's easy to feel compelled to respond promptly amid a steady flood of digital notifications. Setting aside specific periods for these activities allows you to control your interaction with digital gadgets rather than reacting passively to every alarm.

For example, you could check your emails regularly, such as once in the morning, once at lunchtime, and once later in the afternoon. This method allows you to concentrate on your duties without being distracted by incoming emails, which can divide your concentration and impair productivity. It also communicates to your colleagues and contacts when they may expect a response from you, which aids in managing their expectations.

The same holds true for social media. You may avoid wasting time on social media by arranging specific times to read through your accounts. This could mean setting aside a brief time during your lunch break or in the evening to catch up on social media posts. The trick is to ensure these hobbies are separate from your work or personal time.

This systematic approach to digital communication can lessen the impression of being bombarded with information. It lets you interact with digital content on your own terms and prevents you from feeling continuously attached to your devices. Not only does this relieve stress, but it also enables a more meaningful connection with the stuff you consume.

Digital-Free

Creating 'digital-free' zones or periods in your life is a critical barrier that can significantly impact your well-being and relationships. In an age where digital devices are ubiquitous, intentionally establishing areas and periods where technology is not present may be both stimulating and necessary.

Consider making it a rule that no phones are allowed at the dinner table. Meal times can be transformed into opportunities for meaningful connections with your family or housemates with this easy approach. It promotes discussion by allowing people to share their days, opinions, and experiences without being distracted by screens. It's a little change, but it can improve the quality of your conversations and deepen your connections dramatically.

Another effective boundary is to turn off alerts after a particular hour. This could include turning off your phone, closing your laptop, or turning off your tablet at a predetermined time each evening. This border alerts your brain that the workday or time for digital intake has ended, allowing you to unwind and relax. This technique is especially useful for your sleep hygiene since it reduces your exposure to blue light from displays, which can disrupt your sleep patterns.

It would be best if you also considered designating one day each week as a digital detox day. You consciously opt to disconnect from all digital gadgets on this day, giving yourself a total break from emails, social media, and online news. This can be a day to indulge in hobbies, spend time outside, read a book, or enjoy the physical world. A digital detox day can help you re-establish your relationship with technology, minimizing reliance and rejuvenating your perspective.

These digital-free zones and times are about reconnecting with yourself and the people around you, not just withdrawing from technology. They allow you to be more present and involved in the here and now, cultivating a sense of tranquility and awareness that can easily be lost in the digital buzz.

Communications

Setting clear limits with work communication is critical for maintaining a healthy work-life balance, especially in a remote work environment. When your house serves as both your office and your home, it can be difficult for your coworkers – and sometimes even you – to determine when your work begins and ends. Setting and expressing your working hours can help to structure your day.

Begin by establishing your working hours and sharing them with your coworkers. For instance, you may schedule your workday from 9 a.m. until 5 p.m. Make it a practice to refrain from engaging in work-related duties or responding to work-related messages outside of these hours unless it is an emergency. Doing so lets you communicate with your team about when you're available for meetings, phone calls, and email responses.

Utilize tools and features that enforce these boundaries as well. Outside of business hours, many email and messaging systems allow you to set your status to away or offline. You might also configure an automatic out-of-office reply that goes into effect after your workday finishes, alerting senders when they can anticipate your response. This helps control expectations and relieves any internal pressure you may have to face outside of normal working hours.

Maintaining a consistent work schedule is also essential. When your workday is done, physically shut down your work gadgets or close any work-related programs if that isn't possible. This signals to yourself and others that you are no longer on the clock. It may be tempting to check one more email or complete one more assignment, but maintaining boundaries is critical to keeping work from invading your personal life.

Remember that establishing these limits is a continuous process. Understanding how you engage with the digital world and modifying your boundaries as your life and priorities change is a continuous process. It's fine to try different things to see what works best for you. The idea is to establish a digital life that enhances rather than detracts from your total well-being. Taking control of your digital interactions is not only a requirement in our digital age but also a kind of self-care.

NURTURING PERSONAL TIME IN A DIGITAL WORK ENVIRONMENT

Consider how you spend your regular day in the digital world. Most of it is spent in front of a screen, answering emails, attending virtual meetings, and meeting deadlines. While constructive, this digital hustle may be all-consuming. Making time for yourself can seem intimidating, but its value must be manageable. Personal time is more than just a break from work; it is an important aspect of your life where you can engage in activities that will renew and complete you.

Personal time allows you to take a break from the stresses of work and engage in things that bring you genuine joy and relaxation. It might be as simple as reading a book chapter, listening to music, or spending time outdoors. These times offer much-needed reprieve, allowing you to recharge your batteries and detach from the continual assault of digital information.

Engaging in hobbies or activities you are passionate about is also important in developing your time. Painting, cooking, sports, and gardening are not just hobbies; they are outlets for expressing yourself, discovering your creativity, and connecting with what makes you joyful. They provide a sense of accomplishment and fulfillment distinct from professional accomplishments.

Furthermore, this personal time allows for self-reflection and progress. It lets you focus on your ideas, comprehend your emotions, and connect with your inner self. This introspection may illuminate and be grounded, assisting you in maintaining balance and perspective in your life.

Doing Things You Love

Beginning to nurture your personal time entails reconnecting with activities you enjoy but may have put aside. It's easy to lose touch with these basic joys in the buzz of daily life, especially one dominated by digital demands. Consider what you enjoy, especially activities that resonate with your inner self. It may be immersing yourself in the pages of a riveting book, rediscovering the joy of playing a musical instrument, caring for your garden and watching it blossom, or enjoying a leisurely walk in nature and feeling the calm that comes with it.

These activities, frequently seen as hobbies or leisure interests, are far more than mere indulgences or ways to pass the time. They are critical to your mental and emotional wellness. Engaging in these activities provides a much-needed break from the pressures of a job. They let your mind relax and roam, free of the constraints and stress of your professional commitments.

More importantly, these hobbies provide an important counterpoint to the responsibilities of your job life. They provide an environment in which your identity is unrelated to your job or achievements. In these moments, you are not an employee, manager, or business owner; you are an individual with distinct interests and passions. Whether playing a guitar, kneading dough in the kitchen or photographing nature's splendor, these activities allow you to express yourself in ways that work may not.

They also provide a sense of accomplishment and fulfillment distinct from professional success. Completing a difficult trek, creating a picture, or mastering a piece of music can provide a profound sense of personal achievement. This enhances your self-esteem and supports your sense of self outside of your professional life.

Quality Matters

In today's digital age, where screens frequently dominate our attention, it's critical to be careful of the quality of your personal time. Passive activities like browsing the internet or watching television have become commonplace relaxation routines for many people. While they are obviously modes of relaxation, they rarely provide the same revitalizing benefits as more active, engaged pursuits.

Consider how you feel after an hour of looking through social media versus an hour spent engaged in an activity. Painting, writing, sports, and cooking require your full attention and commitment. They draw you into the current moment, requiring active engagement and focus. This kind of involvement
It can be extremely rewarding and energizing. It is a deeper sort of relaxation that not only relieves your mind from the stresses of work but also delivers a sense of accomplishment and delight.

Spending uninterrupted time with family and friends is also essential. In an age when digital distractions abound, being totally present with your loved ones is priceless. This could include eating meals together without the TV or phones, having meaningful talks, or participating in shared activities everyone enjoys.

Being present in the moment lets you relish and experience life's joys. It's about completely listening while someone is speaking, fully immersing yourself in a hobby, or simply enjoying the beauty of a calm afternoon. These experiences enrich your life, offering a much-needed balance in an often fast-paced and digitally-driven society.

Consider scheduling these quality activities at specified times, similar to how you would organize work meetings or appointments. This deliberate allocation of time underlines the significance of these activities in your life. It's a commitment to yourself and your well-being, recognizing that your time is valuable and should be spent with stimulating experiences.

Don't Feel Guilt

Setting aside time for yourself isn't a luxury or an act of selfishness during a rigorous work schedule; it's a necessary habit for your general well-being. It acknowledges that to be efficient and fulfilled in your work life, you must also attend to your personal needs and well-being. This all-encompassing attitude to life ensures that you function and thrive.

Caring for your personal needs may entail drawing clear lines around your work. For example, shutting off work notifications after a specific hour can help you mark the end of your workday. Turning off notifications physically represents the change from work to personal time, allowing you to shift your focus away from professional responsibilities and toward activities that refresh and rejuvenate you.

It is also critical to communicate your availability to your team or colleagues. Notifying them when you'll be taking a break from work-related conversations manages their expectations and confirms your dedication to your personal time. It is about instilling a culture of personal boundaries, which will benefit everyone in the long term.

Balancing work and personal life is especially difficult in an age when technology blurs the distinction between the office and the home. However, by intentionally making time for yourself - whether for hobbies, relaxation, or spending time with loved ones - you convey that your personal life is just as important as your professional one.

CHAPTER 6: DIGITAL DETOX AND MINDFUL TECHNOLOGY USE

The Concept of Digital Detox

As you go about your daily life, surrounded by technology at every turn, the idea of a digital detox may appear appealing and daunting. A digital detox is when you purposefully disconnect from all digital devices, including your smartphone, laptop, tablet, and even your smartwatch. It's about taking a break from the steady stream of emails, social media updates, notifications, and digital noise that consumes so much of your day.

Considering the last time you spent substantial time away from your digital gadgets, it may be scary. In today's society, where cellphones, laptops, and other electronics are nearly extensions of ourselves, disconnecting for an hour or a day can feel like traveling into unknown territory. While these technologies are extremely useful, they have become so embedded in our daily lives that being without them might initially be unnerving.

Taking a vacation from digital devices opens up new avenues for connecting with the world physically and meaningfully. When you take your gaze away from the computer, you're not simply taking a break from technology but also allowing yourself to completely interact with life as it unfolds around you.

Consider taking a walk without your phone. You become more

aware of the small beauties of your surroundings, such as the rustle of leaves, the chatter of birds, and the beautiful patterns of clouds in the sky. These kinds of nuances go undetected while you're engrossed on a digital device. This increased awareness can result in a profound sense of tranquility and a greater appreciation for the world's beauty.

Another part of life that can benefit from digital detox is face-to-face communication. Conversations can become more interesting and meaningful without the distraction of electronics. You may offer your complete focus to the person you're with, resulting in improved understanding and stronger bonds. This level of presence can enhance connections and produce more rewarding interactions.

Furthermore, living without the continual desire to chronicle it for online sharing may be liberating. Enjoying a meal, admiring a sunset, or commemorating a particular occasion becomes less about documenting it for digital consumption and more about the experience itself. This shift in perspective allows you to live more fully in the present moment, resulting in memories that are felt deeply rather than captured superficially.

Taking time away from screens can also help you rediscover life's simple pleasures, such as reading a book, crafts, playing a musical instrument, or simply sitting quietly with your thoughts. These activities provide a particular type of fulfillment sometimes eclipsed by digital media's rapid gratification.

A digital detox can significantly improve your mental and emotional well-being. The urge to stay connected can be difficult in a world where you're constantly blasted with infinite information, notifications, and digital demands. As your mind juggles various streams of information and the constant urge to be responsive, this digital engagement can increase stress and anxiety.

When you intentionally disconnect from this digital barrage, even if only for a little time, you give your mind a much-needed chance to relax and decompress. It's equivalent to giving yourself a tranquil respite from the online world's cacophony and expectations. This pause helps your mind to change attention from external stimulus to internal serenity, assisting in the reduction of mental clutter caused by constant connectivity.

You may notice a steady drop in stress levels throughout a digital detox. When you are not pressured to check emails, respond to messages, or read through social media feeds, your mind may rest, relieving you of the underlying strain these activities can cause. This mental relaxation might also lead to an improvement in mood. As the mental space previously occupied by digital anxieties becomes accessible for more enjoyable and rewarding ideas, you may feel more cheerful, tranquil, and content.

Disconnecting from technology can also improve your general sense of well-being. It gives you time to engage in healing and renewing activities, such as spending time in nature, practicing mindfulness, or engaging in hobbies. These activities can deliver a sense of accomplishment and delight frequently eclipsed by the quick gratification of digital interactions.

Starting a digital detox may appear a big undertaking, but doing so in tiny steps can make the process more doable and less stressful. The aim is to gradually include intervals of disengagement into your routine, allowing you to become accustomed to the feeling.

One good method to start is to set aside an hour each day for a digital detox. This might be during a meal, which can help you appreciate your food more consciously and engage in more meaningful conversations if you're dining with others. You might also designate the hour before bedtime as your time to disengage. This can dramatically enhance your sleep quality since it decreases your exposure to blue light from screens, which has been shown to alter sleep patterns.

As you become more comfortable with these little moments of disengagement, you may increase the duration or frequency. Consider going without digital devices for an entire morning or evening, gradually working up to a full day. Weekends are frequently a good time for a longer digital detox because they provide a break from work-related digital demands. Turn off your electronics and engage in things you enjoy but may ignore during this time. This could include anything from outdoor hobbies such as hiking or cycling to indoor activities such as reading, cooking, or creating.

Finding a rhythm that works for you and fits into your lifestyle is the key to a successful digital detox. It is not about strictly following rules but about striking a balance that feels right for you. Remember that the goal of a digital detox is to take a break from constant digital connectedness, not to add another source of stress to your life.

As your digital detox progresses, you may look forward to these disengagement intervals. They can become treasured moments in which you deeply reconnect with yourself and the world around you. You may include digital detoxes into your life to improve your general well-being by finding a strategy that works for you.

MINDFULNESS IN THE AGE OF DISTRACTION

As you go about your daily life surrounded by continual digital buzz, adopting more mindfulness practices into your interactions with technology can dramatically improve your capacity to manage these distractions. Mindfulness, or the discipline of being completely present and engaged in the present moment, can change how you use and interpret technology, transforming potential distractions into instruments for productivity and connection.

Begin by becoming more conscious of your digital behaviors. Consider how often you reach for your phone without a stated reason. Is it a reflexive movement during boredom or a halt in activity? Simply being aware of these patterns allows you to begin changing them. Pause every time you feel the impulse to check your device. Take a deep breath and consider, "Is this necessary right now, or can it wait?" This little moment of mindfulness can help you interrupt the pattern of compulsive checking and use technology more intentionally.

When you utilize your electronics, aim to do so with complete awareness. For example, when checking emails, give it your full attention and resist the temptation to multitask. This focused approach increases your efficiency and relieves the tension of being scattered and overwhelmed by various duties.

Designating distinct 'tech-free' zones or times throughout your day is also useful. This could occur during meals, the first hour after waking up, or an hour before bedtime. During these moments, consciously engage in non-screen activities like reading a book, meditating, or conversing with a family member. These pauses are vital for clearing your thoughts and minimizing reliance on digital stimulation.

Also, think about the emotional impact of your technological use. Pay attention to how different forms of material affect your emotions. Find that specific websites, applications, or social media platforms often make you feel worried, stressed, or down. It may be time to reassess how you interact with them. Choose to consume stuff that motivates and inspires you, improving your mental and emotional well-being.

Here are strategies you can employ:

Set Specific Purposes for Technology Use: In a world where digital devices provide limitless possibilities, it's easy to become distracted. Before using any device, ask yourself, "What is my intention here?" This method can significantly alter how you engage with technology. If you take up your phone to respond to an essential message, do so and then put it away. If you're using your computer for business, fight the impulse to engage in other internet activity. Setting a defined purpose can help you stay focused, making your use of technology more intentional rather than aimless browsing or procrastination.

Use Technology Mindfully for Learning and Creativity: Instead of wasting time scrolling through social media or binge-watching TV series, use your screen time to engage in enriching activities. This might be anything from online classes that help you improve your professional skills to creative apps that express your artistic side. For example, spend your evenings or leisure time writing a blog, creating digital artwork, or composing music. Listen to podcasts that help you understand the world or teach something new. This increases the productivity of your online time and is more enjoyable and stimulating for your intellectual and creative growth.

Mindful Notification Management: In today's world of continual connectedness, notifications can distract and fragment your attention. Begin by reviewing the notifications on your phone and computer. Turn off notifications from apps that are not necessary or valuable in your daily life. This might include social media apps, specific news apps, or any other app that routinely sends you push notifications. Decide on specific times to check your emails or texts, such as in the morning, during lunch, and again in the evening. Doing so lets you regain control of your attention and minimize the constant tug on it. This attentive approach to notification management can help you stay more present in real-life activities and interactions, resulting in more attention, less stress, and a more balanced daily routine.

Practice Gratitude for Technology: When you're feeling frustrated with digital overload, it can help to adjust your viewpoint and consider the benefits of technology. Take some time to think about how technology has made your life easier and more connected. It could be how your smartphone connects you with loved ones, how online tools have enabled you to work from home, or the convenience of accessing a wealth of information at your fingertips. This practice of gratitude can transform your relationship with technology from one of dependency or annoyance to one of appreciation and beneficial use. Recognizing the benefits and conveniences of technology might help you see your gadgets as helpful tools that support your lifestyle and goals rather than distractions. This mindset shift can lead to a more balanced and positive attitude toward technology.

Mindful Breathing Before Using Devices: Before starting a session on your phone, laptop, or tablet, take a moment to practice mindful breathing. Spend a few minutes breathing deeply and slowly in and out. This simple activity can help you concentrate your thoughts, providing peace and purpose to your next internet contact. Doing so establishes a mental barrier between your non-digital life and the digital task at hand. This pause can help you become more aware of your motives for using the device and avoid unthinking, mindless use. It's a means of refreshing your mind, ensuring that you do it with intention and attention when you use technology.

Digital Mindfulness Meditation: Set aside time for brief meditation sessions that explicitly address your relationship with technology. During these sessions, ponder quietly on your digital habits. Consider how technology influences your mood, stress levels, and productivity. Is there a pattern of use that routinely causes anxiety or dissatisfaction? Are there any apps or activities that encourage or inspire you? This thoughtful reflection will help you become more conscious of how you use digital devices and how they affect your life. With this enhanced awareness, you may make more intentional decisions about how you use technology, steering it in beneficial directions for your well-being. Digital mindfulness meditation can be an effective strategy for establishing healthier, more balanced digital habits.

Physical clues for awareness: Try incorporating physical clues into your digital surroundings to help you retain awareness while using technology. This may be a simple sticker on your phone, a note next to your computer, or even a specific wallpaper on your desktop. These cues are mild reminders to remain alert when using your smartphone. When you encounter this sticker or note, use it as a reminder to swiftly assess your current state of mind. Ask yourself questions such as, "Am I using this device purposefully right now?" and "How do I feel at this moment?" This practice can help you become more aware of your digital habits and encourage you to utilize technology to benefit your mental and emotional well-being.

Technology Sabbaticals: Consider taking regular breaks from technology. This could entail devoting a weekend, a day, or even a few hours to being fully disconnected from digital devices. During this moment, immerse yourself in the physical realm. Participate in activities you enjoy but may have overlooked, such as reading a physical book, experiencing the outdoors, practicing a hobby, or spending undisturbed time with family and friends. These breaks are about more than just what you're leaving behind; they're also about what you're entering: a space where you can reconnect with yourself and your environment without the distractions of technology. These sabbaticals can help you reset your relationship with digital devices, lessening your reliance and renewing your perspective on how you use technology in everyday life.

Mindful Content Consumption: Content constantly competes for your attention in today's digital age. Make an attempt to be more selective about what you eat. Choose to interact with sites that are encouraging, instructive, or inspirational. Be mindful of how various forms of content influence your mood and overall well-being. Discover that specific websites, social media platforms, or media types leave you exhausted, stressed, or sad. It may be time to reconsider your consumption patterns. Choose stuff that improves your life and corresponds with your personal ideals.

Reflection Time After Using Technology: After using technology, whether for work or enjoyment, take a few moments to reflect on your experiences. Ask yourself questions like, "Did using this device or platform add value to my day?" or, "Did I stick to my plan or get sidetracked?" This reflection is a type of self-check-in that helps you become more conscious of your digital behaviors. It enables you to identify patterns in your technology use, whether productive, distracting, or somewhere between. This mindful exercise helps you to consider the role technology plays in your life and whether it is consistent with your overall goals and well-being. Taking these minutes to reflect allows you to make more educated decisions about using technology in the future, resulting in a healthier and more balanced relationship with your digital gadgets.

EMBRACING
SLOW TECH FOR
A FULLER LIFE

As you go about your everyday life, surrounded by the fast-paced world of technology, have you ever considered adopting the 'Slow Tech' concept for a more fulfilling, balanced life?

Slow Tech is a notion that urges you to reconsider your relationship with technology, pushing you to use it mindfully and intentionally. It is about accepting that while technology can substantially improve your life, it should not control it. This strategy focuses on developing a rhythm with your devices that aligns with your personal beliefs and supports the life you want to live.

Consider how technology currently fits into your life. Does it feel like it's improving your experiences, or does it frequently leave you feeling rushed, distracted, or overwhelmed? Slow Tech provides an alternative method. It's about using technology to help you achieve your goals, not as a constant source of pleasure or distraction. Instead of mindlessly browsing social media, you may use your phone to connect meaningfully with friends and family, learn a new skill, or help with daily duties.

Embracing Slow Tech entails placing limits on your usage of technology. It's about actively determining when and how you use your devices. This could include scheduling specific times of day to check your email and social media and setting up specified times to put your devices away, such as during family meals or before bedtime. It's about being present in the moment and not allowing your digital devices to distract you from real-life events.

Slow Tech also supports the principle of quality over quantity. It opts to engage with fewer digital channels but more meaningfully and gratifyingly. It's about choosing apps and websites that truly offer value to your life, whether they're informative, motivating, or simply enjoyable, rather than those that waste your time and energy.

To begin your Slow Tech adventure, take a step back and consider how you now engage with digital gadgets. Begin by observing your regular activities and behaviors. How often do you grab your smartphone, tablet, or laptop? What motivated you to do so? Are your interactions with these gadgets mostly planned, or do you check them without a stated reason?

Consider identifying particular periods when you could minimize your technology use. For example, you may read a book instead of scrolling through social media or viewing videos online in the evening. This not only takes your eyes away from devices but also allows your mind to engage in a new, often more pleasant, activity. Reading can be a great way to relax, develop creativity, and prepare for a good night's sleep.

Mealtimes are another opportunity to embrace Slow Tech. Try to avoid using your phone or other digital gadgets during meals. This allows you to thoroughly immerse yourself in eating, savoring your meal, and enjoying their companionship if you're with others. It's about being in the moment, enjoying the flavors of your food, and engaging in discussion around the table. This approach improves your dining experience and helps you connect with loved ones.

These tiny modifications in your everyday routine can greatly influence your overall health. By intentionally reducing your use of technology at particular times, you free up time for more meaningful and stimulating activities. It's about striking a balance where technology has its place but only consumes your time and attention.

As you adopt Slow Tech concepts, consider the quality of your digital engagements. Every interaction with technology can affect your well-being favorably and badly. Take a moment to consider how you feel after spending time online. Do your digital activities leave you feeling inspired, educated, and revitalized, or do you frequently feel exhausted, nervous, or dissatisfied?

Evaluating the quality of your digital interactions entails examining the types of content you consume and the activities you participate in online. Are you spending time on websites or social media platforms that promote personal development, or are they sources of negativity and comparison? Slow Tech encourages you to curate your digital environment, just as your physical surroundings, to support and enhance your life.

Consider following online communities or people who inspire and motivate you. Surround yourself with digital content that reflects your interests and goals, whether personal development, a hobby, or professional advancement. Use applications to help you learn new skills and knowledge. This might include language learning apps, educational platforms, or technologies that boost creativity. Engaging with content promoting growth and pleasure can shift your relationship with technology from passive consumption to active enrichment.

Also, consider limiting your digital interactions. Consider limiting the time you spend on specific activities in your daily life, just as you would with your internet activities. Limit your time spent on platforms or programs that don't provide value to your life. This could be utilizing a timer on social media or establishing designated days or periods when you entirely withdraw from certain digital networks.

Embracing Slow Tech also entails being comfortable with not replying to communications immediately or not being always available. It acknowledges that it is acceptable to take the time to reply carefully or disengage from digital gadgets to reconnect with the world around you - to listen, observe, and enjoy life's basic pleasures.

Remember that adopting a Slow Tech approach is a personal journey that requires deciding how technology fits into your life. It's about striking a balance that allows you to get the benefits of technology while appreciating the richness of a more focused, purposeful lifestyle. Slow Tech can help you live a richer, happier life in which technology serves you rather than vice versa.

CHAPTER 7: RAISING CHILDREN IN THE DIGITAL AGE

Digital Impact on Young Minds

As you navigate the world of parenting in the digital era, it's critical to understand how internet exposure can influence your children's and teens' developing minds. The digital world is an important aspect of their life, far more than it was for past generations, and it presents both opportunities and challenges.

Consider how your child or teen interacts with digital devices. They are more than simply entertainment tools; they also serve as gateways to a wealth of information, social interaction, and learning opportunities. However, the digital world provides a unique set of stimuli that can impact their growth, conduct, and mental well-being.

Over Stimulation

The constant stream of digital information and stimuli that children and adolescents are exposed to can significantly impact their developing brains. The rapid-fire nature of digital content, such as social media feeds and fast-paced video games, can substantially impact their cognitive and emotional development.

One of the primary areas of concern is attention span. Many digital platforms require fast satisfaction and quick shifts of focus, which might decrease the capacity to concentrate on tasks for extended periods. This is especially important for children and adolescents whose attention and concentration abilities are still growing. Their brains are wired in an environment where quick material consumption is the norm, which may limit their capacity to engage deeply and maintain attention on slower-paced, more demanding tasks.

Creativity may also be impaired. While digital media can be a valuable source of inspiration, excessive screen time can result in the passive intake of content rather than active, inventive interaction. Children may need help to engage in creative play and generate original ideas if they spend most of their leisure time getting information rather than creating.

Furthermore, excessive screen use, particularly before bedtime, might alter sleeping patterns. The blue light emitted by screens interferes with the generation of melatonin, the hormone that regulates sleep. Poor sleep can harm academic performance, mood, and overall health.

Social skills are another area where technology has a huge impact. While online platforms can be useful for socializing, particularly for connecting with individuals who share similar interests, they must partially duplicate the nuances of in-person encounters. The nuances of body language, tone of voice, and real-time emotional responses are critical components of communication that are sometimes overlooked in digital interactions. As a result, too much screen time can impede the development of these important interpersonal skills.

Social Media

Social media has a multifaceted function in the lives of teenagers, providing both pleasant and challenging experiences. On the one hand, it gives a platform for self-expression and a means of connecting with others, which can be especially useful during adolescence, a period of identity exploration and social development. Teens may express themselves, share their interests, and join groups of like-minded people. This can be uplifting and validating, allowing kids to develop a feeling of self and belonging.

However, the downside of social networking is its ability to cause worry and pressure. One of the major issues is kids' propensity to compare themselves to the frequently idealized depictions of others' lives that they encounter online. Social media feeds are flooded with expertly selected images and postings that portray an unrealistic quality of life, looks, and achievement. This can lead to feelings of inadequacy and low self-esteem, as teenagers may believe that their own lives do not compare to the supposedly wonderful lives they witness on their screens.

Furthermore, the desire for likes, comments, and followers might measure self-esteem and popularity. This might create persistent pressure to produce appealing or popular information, resulting in a loop of seeking validation and approval on social media. The temporary high of receiving likes or good remarks can swiftly devolve into anxiety and self-doubt if the expected confirmation does not arrive.

Social media can also increase feelings of exclusion or loneliness. Teens may feel excluded when they see posts about social groups or activities to which they were not invited. This 'fear of missing out' (FOMO) can intensify feelings of loneliness and increase social media use to feel connected, resulting in a vicious cycle.

Giving Guidance

As a parent in this digital age, one of your primary responsibilities is to guide your child through their digital adventure. This entails more than just limiting their screen time or implementing parental controls. It's about having open and continuing conversations with your child about their internet experiences and helping them comprehend the intricacies of the digital world.

Encourage your youngster to discuss what they see online. This might include everything from the videos kids view to their interactions on social media platforms. Create a safe and open environment for these discussions without judgment and instant censure. This method encourages children to tell you about their online experiences, including any concerns or uncertainties they may have.

Help children realize the difference between the online world and real life. Children and teenagers must understand that what they see online may not always be a true reflection of reality. Discuss how online content can be modified, updated, or presented in a way that draws attention to or promotes specific ideas. Encouraging critical thinking can help children gain a more balanced and educated view of what they see online.

Another critical part is to educate kids about online privacy and the dangers of disclosing personal information. Explain how seemingly innocent information can be used in unexpected or undesirable ways. Discuss the long-term consequences of their digital footprint, such as how what they publish now may be seen by others in the future, including possible employers or educational institutions.

It is also critical to teach kids about recognizing and respecting the privacy of others. Please encourage them to reflect before sharing or posting something about someone else and recognize consent's significance in these instances.

Remember that guiding your child's digital path is an ongoing process. It entails remaining current on the newest trends and issues in the digital realm, being willing to learn and adapt, and, most importantly, establishing an ongoing dialogue with your child. You can help kids navigate the online world safely, informed, and respectfully by playing an active and supporting role in their digital lives.

PARENTAL GUIDANCE AND BOUNDARIES

As a parent in this ever-changing digital world, guiding your child's digital usage is important in helping them develop into well-rounded people. It is about establishing boundaries that safeguard kids while teaching them how to use technology safely and consciously. This instruction is especially essential in reducing the anxiety that might result from excessive or unmonitored internet intake.

Limitations

Establishing clear rules and boundaries for internet usage is critical in controlling your child's involvement with technology. This entails developing an organized strategy that defines when and how devices can be used, particularly for leisure and enjoyment. For example, you may specify that certain times of day are device-free. This might occur during family meals, which can then become opportunities for conversation and connection without the distraction of electronics. These moments allow everyone to focus on one another, resulting in deeper family relationships.

Another important barrier would be restricting screen time before bedtime. Encouraging your child to put away digital gadgets at least an hour before bedtime will help them sleep better. Instead of using devices during this pre-sleep period, encourage activities like reading, listening to soothing music, or family storytelling. This promotes better sleep and builds a relaxing nighttime ritual, which is critical for their overall health and wellbeing.

Establishing and following these standards contributes to a well-balanced digital environment in your household. It educates your youngster that, while technology has its uses, it should not control all aspects of life. These boundaries guarantee that digital device use is integrated into your family's routine in a healthy, controlled manner rather than becoming an ongoing presence.

These regulations must be communicated clearly and consistently and explain why they exist. Understanding why these boundaries exist might help your child view them as logical and necessary rather than arbitrary constraints. Furthermore, be prepared to modify these guidelines as your child grows and their needs and circumstances shift. What works for a young child may not be appropriate for a teen, so being adaptable and attentive to their changing needs is essential.

Their Digital Side

Active participation in your child's digital world is an important facet of parenting in the digital age. It's about becoming interested in the platforms, apps, and content that hold your child's attention. This involvement does not require you to monitor every click or hover over them whenever they are online. Instead, show genuine interest in their online activities and experiences and cultivate an open and trusting connection in which they feel comfortable sharing their digital world with you.

Begin by familiarizing yourself with the platforms and apps that your youngster utilizes. You don't have to become an expert, but having a basic grasp can allow you to participate in more informed and meaningful discussions. Ask your child to show you their favorite apps, games, or websites and explain what they enjoy about them. This can be a fun and instructive way to engage with your child and view the digital world from their perspective.

Encourage talks regarding the content kids discover online

as you learn more about their activities. Discuss what they find intriguing or entertaining and anything that concerns or confuses them. These chats can help teach your child critical thinking skills, particularly distinguishing between trustworthy and untrustworthy online material.

Discussing how to deal with unfavorable content or events is also important. Like the real world, the internet can bring problems, and your child should understand how to navigate them securely and ethically. This could include discussions about cyberbullying, discovering inappropriate content, or realizing the permanence of what they post online.

By taking an interest in your child's digital environment, you keep an eye on their online activities and foster trust and openness. It conveys that you are there to support and guide them, not impose rules and limits. This strategy can help your child develop a healthy and responsible attitude toward technology and the skills and information needed to safely and successfully navigate the digital world.

Emotional Impact

Encouraging open communication regarding the emotional consequences of internet usage is an important element of guiding your child through their online environment. The digital landscape is rich with content that can elicit many emotions, from joy and excitement to dread and bewilderment. Your youngster must understand that being emotionally influenced by what they see online is normal.

Create an environment where your child feels comfortable addressing how online interactions and content affect them. This may be discussing a video that made them laugh, a news report that baffled them, or a social media message that made them feel excluded or inadequate. Validate their emotions by actively listening and demonstrating empathy. Tell them it's alright to feel a certain way and that they're not alone in their experiences.

Help them understand that most of what they see online is selected and that individuals frequently only share their finest moments, which aren't usually representative of real life. This can help them gain a more balanced perspective on social media and lessen emotions of inadequacy or jealousy.

Also, utilize these interactions to educate your child on managing their emotions in response to digital media. Discuss ways to deal with unpleasant feelings, such as taking breaks from specific platforms, using technology wisely, or engaging in activities that improve their mood. Teach kids they have control over their digital experiences, including disconnecting from disturbing content.

Encourage children to come to you with any concerns or questions about what they learn online. Whether it's concern about a news story, discomfort from a social contact, or anything else, knowing they can turn to a trustworthy adult may be extremely reassuring.

Role Model

It is quite effective to model the digital behavior you want your youngster to exhibit. Children are great observers and frequently mimic their parents' or guardians' mannerisms and routines. As a result, how you treat technology greatly impacts your digital habits and attitudes.

Show a balanced approach to your personal internet usage. Allow your child to see that while you may use technology for business, staying informed, or staying in touch with friends and family, you also value time away from screens. Make it a practice to put your phone away during family meals, demonstrating that you value this time for connection and conversation. Alternatively, schedule times when you will not check emails or social media, such as during family activities or weekend mornings. This demonstrates to your youngster that, while technology is a valuable tool, it does not have to rule all aspects of your life.

Get involved in offline activities and invite your youngster to join you. This could include everything from outdoor activities, reading books, cooking together, or participating in a hobby. These activities not only help to balance screen time but also provide opportunities for bonding and skill development.

It's also crucial to consider how you communicate about technology and its significance in your life. Avoid continually expressing anger over being reliant on your phone or computer for work, as this can send conflicting signals about the role of technology. Instead, please talk about the benefits of technology and the significance of taking breaks from it for mental health and wellbeing.

Setting a good example with your own technological habits teaches your child valuable lessons about balance, self-regulation, and the importance of the world beyond screens. Your actions can motivate children to build a healthy relationship with technology, in which kids acknowledge its benefits while also understanding the significance of disconnecting and participating with the physical world around them. This balanced approach is critical for their general growth and wellbeing, allowing children to mature into well-rounded individuals capable of navigating the digital and physical worlds with confidence and mindfulness.

BUILDING DIGITAL RESILIENCE IN KIDS

As you guide your child through their digital adventure, digital resilience is one of the most significant gifts you can bestow. In an ever-connected world, where the digital environment is always changing, teaching your child how to navigate online areas securely and successfully is critical. It is about preparing students to confront the challenges of the digital world while taking advantage of its numerous opportunities for learning and growth.

Content
Developing digital resilience in your child begins with open and honest discussions about the online environment. It is critical to sit down with your child and discuss the wide range of content they may encounter online. The internet is like a vast city with various neighborhoods: some are lovely and enlightening, while others may be misleading or destructive.

Make children understand that not all online stuff is created equal. Some websites and social media posts aim to enlighten and educate, while others may be prejudiced, erroneous, or intended to deceive. Teach them to recognize the differences. Encourage children to reflect critically on what they read and see online. Inquire, "Who created this content?" and "What might be their motive?" This teaches kids to take only some pieces of information at face value.

Discuss with them the concept of 'fake news' and how certain things on the internet might be exaggerated or fully created for various reasons. Emphasize the significance of double-checking information using credible sources before adopting it as fact. Verification is an essential ability for creating digital resilience.

It is also beneficial to teach them that the internet, like any other element of life, necessitates discretion and careful navigation. Encourage them to contact you or another trusted adult if they come across something they are unsure about. Tell them it's alright to have questions and that you're here to help them discover the answers.

Interactions

Discussing online interactions is important for guiding your child through the digital world. Just as in the real world, how kids interact with others online can have a big impact. It is critical to help them grasp the complexities of Internet communication and the social dynamics that accompany it.

Begin by discussing the value of courteous interaction in digital places. Remind them that behind each profile, remark, and message is a real person with emotions. Encourage children to speak online like they would in person, with kindness and respect. Discuss how words can be strong and deeply impact individuals, particularly when there is no face-to-face interaction to judge reactions and feelings.

Address cyberbullying head-on. Explain to your child what cyberbullying is and how it might present itself, such as through harsh remarks and texts, spreading rumors, or publishing humiliating images of someone without their permission. Make it clear that such behavior is inappropriate and will result in serious consequences. Teach children how to spot cyberbullying indicators in their and their classmates' interactions. Provide them with strategies for responding if they witness or experience something. This could involve avoiding responding to the bully, preserving evidence, and reporting the behavior to a trusted adult.

It's also critical to promote empathy in their online conversations. Help them understand how to put themselves in the shoes of others and how their words and actions may influence them. Encourage them to be an upstander who speaks out against bullying and helps people being attacked.

Discuss the value of privacy and ponder before sharing personal information or data about others. Explain how difficult or impossible it is to return something once it has been shared online.

Challenges

Teaching your child how to respond to online obstacles is important to developing their digital resilience. The online world, like the real world, can provide a range of obstacles, and it is critical that your child feels prepared and supported as they face them.

Begin by describing the various types of problematic situations they may experience online. This could involve encountering unsettling or inappropriate content, receiving harsh or nasty comments, or being pressured by peers to participate in activities they are uncomfortable with. Children must understand that, while tragic, these incidents are not uncommon in the digital age.

Explain to your youngster that how they react to these events can greatly impact the result. Teach children that it is acceptable to avoid disturbing content and to block or report users who are hurtful or inappropriate. Emphasize the significance of avoiding responding to negative comments or peer pressure, as doing so can aggravate the situation.

Encourage open communication. Inform children that they can always come to you or another trusted adult if they encounter something online that makes them uncomfortable, worried, or doubtful. Assure them that asking for help demonstrates strength, not weakness. Create a safe environment for these chats, free of judgment and quick consequences, so they feel comfortable sharing their online experiences with you.

Discuss how to deal with these difficulties. This could involve taking a vacation from a specific app or website, explaining how to report inappropriate information or conduct to the platform, or developing good methods to deal with peer pressure. They must believe they have strategies and help to navigate these situations.

Disconnection

Building your child's digital resilience entails more than just teaching them how to navigate online environments; it also includes encouraging them to connect and engage in the world outside screens regularly. Helping your child understand and appreciate the importance of taking breaks from the digital world is critical to their mental and emotional well-being.

Explain to your youngster that, like any other activity, it is vital to strike a balance when using technology. Encourage kids to take regular breaks from their devices and to engage in offline activities. This could include anything from outdoor activities and reading books to hobbies such as painting, cooking, and music. These activities provide a healthy break from screens and help with their general development, such as physical fitness, creativity, and cognitive skills.

Developing a love of the environment and outdoor activities can be especially beneficial. Hiking, motorcycling, or even a simple walk in the park can provide a welcome break from the digital world. It allows kids to explore, learn, and interact with the natural world while providing experiences that cannot be reproduced online.

Encourage family activities that do not include screens. This could include board games, family cooking nights, and storytelling sessions. These shared events can enhance family bonds and generate long-lasting memories, demonstrating to your youngster that meaningful and enjoyable interactions can occur outside digital gadgets.

Help them understand how withdrawing from the digital world allows them to reconnect with themselves and their environment. It allows individuals to contemplate, relax, and engage in mindfulness activities, all of which are beneficial to their mental and emotional health.

By teaching your child the value of balancing their digital and offline lives, you are allowing them to realize that life is full and satisfying beyond digital environments. This balance is critical for establishing a well-rounded outlook on life and guaranteeing long-term well-being in an increasingly digital world.

Building digital resilience in your child involves empowering them to navigate the digital environment confidently and mindfully rather than instilling fear. By giving them the necessary knowledge, resources, and support, you are assisting them in developing the resilience that will serve them well both online and in real life.

CONCLUSION

As you consider the future, remember that the digital landscape constantly changes, bringing new trends and possible pressures. Understanding these new digital trends will be essential for navigating this ever-changing environment. The rapid pace of technology development can be both exhilarating and overwhelming, but by being aware and adaptive, you can efficiently manage these changes while maintaining your resilience.

Artificial intelligence (AI) and augmented reality (AR) are rapidly emerging fields that will increasingly integrate into everyday life. These improvements promise to open up many new possibilities, revolutionizing how you work, study, and connect with the world around you.

Artificial intelligence is expected to advance, potentially automating many areas of daily living and providing personalized experiences ranging from smart homes to tailored health suggestions. Augmented reality can transform how you interact with your surroundings by superimposing digital information on the actual world and improving educational, entertaining, and professional experiences.

However, these wonderful improvements bring challenges that you should be aware of. More integrated digital interactions may result in more data being gathered and processed, raising privacy and security issues. It is critical to keep aware of how your data is being used and understand the privacy rules of your devices and platforms.

Overwhelming information is another difficulty. As technology becomes increasingly integrated into your life, the amount of information you are exposed to might skyrocket. Learning to filter this information and focus on what is relevant and useful to you will be an essential skill.

Staying current on these changes necessitates actively seeking out information and resources. This could include monitoring tech news, engaging in online forums, attending webinars, and discussing developing technology. Understanding the possible impact of these breakthroughs can help you better prepare to adapt to and use them to enrich your life.

It's perfectly reasonable to feel excited and nervous as you enter the future and confront the plethora of new technology it provides. Every innovation has its own learning curve, and allowing yourself to explore it at your own pace is critical. Remember, the goal isn't to become an expert on every new item or platform. Instead, consider how these technical advancements may improve your life and correspond with your unique values and aspirations.

Each new piece of technology has the potential to provide benefits, such as making some chores easier, improving your capacity to connect with others, or opening up new opportunities for learning and pleasure. However, it is equally critical to be cautious and deliberate about the technologies you include in your life. Ask yourself: Does this technology improve my life in a meaningful way? Is it consistent with my priorities and values? By answering these questions, you can choose to interact with technology in a way that enhances your life without feeling compelled to follow every new fad.

Adapting to technological advances entails knowing their effects on mental and emotional well-being. As the digital world gets more deep and engaging, it's more crucial than ever to strike a good balance between your online and offline lives. It's easy to become engrossed in the digital current, but remember to also root yourself in the real world.

Set boundaries for yourself when using digital devices. This could include scheduling particular times for accessing emails and social media, turning off notifications during family or personal leisure time, or even declaring tech-free zones in your house. Try to engage in non-screen-related activities, such as reading a book, pursuing a hobby, spending time in nature, or simply enjoying quiet moments of thought.

Staying adaptable and open-minded is critical in a rapidly evolving world of digital technology. Embracing change, rather than opposing it, can transform the technology innovation experience from a problem to one of growth and learning. Your adaptability is valuable in managing these changes, keeping you current and informed.

Continuously learning about new technology and digital trends is a proactive strategy to stay ahead. In today's environment, there are countless resources for learning and remaining informed. Online courses provide knowledge in various industries, allowing you to explore specific areas of interest, such as the most recent developments in AI, cybersecurity, and digital marketing. These courses frequently offer a combination of academic knowledge and practical application, making them an excellent method to learn new skills or improve existing ones.

Webinars and podcasts are other useful resources. They can provide insights from tech industry professionals and thought leaders, bringing you up to date on the newest developments and predictions for the future. This is especially beneficial for comprehending the broader ramifications of technological breakthroughs and how they may affect society, your work, or your personal life.

Reading up on the most recent internet trends is also essential. This could happen via tech news websites, blogs, or industry publications. Staying current on technological breakthroughs, controversies, and ethical considerations allows you to better grasp the ever-changing digital landscape. It also prepares you to have educated conversations in both professional and personal settings.

As you traverse the digital world, remember that how you utilize digital technologies can greatly impact your mental health. I advise you to utilize these technologies safely and attentively, ensuring that your internet connections improve, not subtract from, your overall psychological health.

Being cautious about the stuff you engage with online is an important step toward using digital tools responsibly for your mental health. The internet is a large space packed with a variety of stuff, not all of which is good for your mental health. Select platforms and resources that encourage, motivate, or educate you. This could include websites and apps that provide positive news, instructional stuff, or content relevant to your hobbies and interests.

Conversely, be mindful of how websites or social media platforms make you feel. If you find that spending time on a specific platform often makes you feel nervous, stressed, or overwhelmed, it may be time to reassess how much time you spend there or whether you should visit it. Remember that the stuff you consume has the potential to influence your mood and attitude, and making deliberate decisions about what you consume can have a significant impact on your overall well-being.

Setting limits on your internet intake is equally crucial. It is simple to become constantly linked in the digital era, but this constant connectedness can lead to digital fatigue. To avoid this, set apart distinct periods in your day to check social media, send emails, and browse the internet. This may include avoiding checking emails first thing in the morning, setting off time in the afternoon for social media, or implementing a no-screens policy an hour before bedtime.

Sticking to these boundaries will help you manage your screen time and enjoy the benefits of the digital world without it taking over your life. These limitations also allow you to engage in offline activities that promote mental health, such as reading, exercising, or spending time with loved ones. Maintaining a balance between your online and offline activities will ensure that your digital life contributes to your general mental health and happiness rather than detracting from it.

Moreover, make sure to arrange time for digital detoxes. You can take these breaks at shorter intervals during the day or at longer intervals, such as on the weekends when you switch off all of your electronic devices. You should make use of this time to engage in activities that are beneficial to your mental health, such as spending leisure time in nature, engaging in mindfulness practices, or pursuing hobbies.

In order to actively aid your mental health, it is important to remember to use technology. Meditation, stress management, and self-care are all topics that may be addressed through the use of a variety of apps and online services. Your mental health may be preserved with the help of these tools, which can also provide you with direction and support while you go about your daily activities.

Last, but not least, keep in mind that technology should work for you, not the other way around. Making intelligent and conscientious use of digital technologies can assist you in preserving a positive mental state and lead to a life that contains a greater sense of equilibrium. Stay informed and engaged, but the most important thing is to maintain your health.